IMPROVING INTERGROUP RELATIONS
AMONG YOUTH

SUMMARY OF A RESEARCH WORKSHOP

Forum on Adolescence

Board on Children, Youth, and Families
Commission on Behavioral and Social Sciences and Education

National Research Council
and
Institute of Medicine

NATIONAL ACADEMY PRESS
Washington, D.C.

NATIONAL ACADEMY PRESS 2101 Constitution Avenue, N.W. Washington, D.C. 20418

NOTICE: The project that is the subject of this report was approved by the Governing Board of the National Research Council, whose members are drawn from the councils of the National Academy of Sciences, the National Academy of Engineering, and the Institute of Medicine. The members of the committee responsible for the report were chosen for their special competences and with regard for appropriate balance.

The study was supported by Grant No 99-10301 between the National Academy of Sciences and Carnegie Corporation of New York. Any opinions, findings, conclusions, or recommendations expressed in this publication are those of the author(s) and do not necessarily reflect the view of the organizations or agencies that provided support for this project.

THE NATIONAL ACADEMIES

National Academy of Sciences
National Academy of Engineering
Institute of Medicine
National Research Council

The **National Academy of Sciences** is a private, nonprofit, self-perpetuating society of distinguished scholars engaged in scientific and engineering research, dedicated to the furtherance of science and technology and to their use for the general welfare. Upon the authority of the charter granted to it by the Congress in 1863, the Academy has a mandate that requires it to advise the federal government on scientific and technical matters. Dr. Bruce M. Alberts is president of the National Academy of Sciences.

The **National Academy of Engineering** was established in 1964, under the charter of the National Academy of Sciences, as a parallel organization of outstanding engineers. It is autonomous in its administration and in the selection of its members, sharing with the National Academy of Sciences the responsibility for advising the federal government. The National Academy of Engineering also sponsors engineering programs aimed at meeting national needs, encourages education and research, and recognizes the superior achievements of engineers. Dr. William A. Wulf is president of the National Academy of Engineering.

The **Institute of Medicine** was established in 1970 by the National Academy of Sciences to secure the services of eminent members of appropriate professions in the examination of policy matters pertaining to the health of the public. The Institute acts under the responsibility given to the National Academy of Sciences by its congressional charter to be an adviser to the federal government and, upon its own initiative, to identify issues of medical care, research, and education. Dr. Kenneth I. Shine is president of the Institute of Medicine.

The **National Research Council** was organized by the National Academy of Sciences in 1916 to associate the broad community of science and technology with the Academy's purposes of furthering knowledge and advising the federal government. Functioning in accordance with general policies determined by the Academy, the Council has become the principal operating agency of both the National Academy of Sciences and the National Academy of Engineering in providing services to the government, the public, and the scientific and engineering communities. The Council is administered jointly by both Academies and the Institute of Medicine. Dr. Bruce M. Alberts and Dr. William A. Wulf are chairman and vice chairman, respectively, of the National Research Council.

Michele D. Kipke, *Director*
Zodie E. Makonnen, *Associate Director*
Amy Gawad, *Senior Project Assistant*
Elena Nightingale, *Adviser*

PARTICIPANTS
WORKSHOP ON RESEARCH TO IMPROVE INTERGROUP
RELATIONS AMONG YOUTH

DAVID HAMBURG (*Chair*), Carnegie Corporation of New York
(President Emeritus)

DENNIS J. BARR, Facing History and Ourselves, Cambridge,
Massachusetts

REBECCA BLANK, Council of Economic Advisers, Washington, D.C.

KELLY BRILLIANT, Program for Young Negotiators, Cambridge,
Massachusetts

PHYLLIS C. BROWN, Lesley College

DAVID CAMPT, President's Initiative on Race, Washington, D.C.

CINDY CARLSON, University of Texas, Austin

KENYON CHAN, Loyola Marymount University

CAMILLE ZUBRINSKY CHARLES, University of Pennsylvania

BARBARA COLLINS, Education Training and Research Associates,
Santa Cruz, California

CONSTANCE FLANAGAN, Pennsylvania State University

MICHELE FOSTER, Claremont Graduate University

EUGENE GARCIA, University of California, Berkeley

SHERRYL BROWNE GRAVES, Hunter College, City University of
New York

PATRICIA MARKS GREENFIELD, University of California,
Los Angeles

DIANE HUGHES, New York University

PHYLLIS A. KATZ, Institute for Research on Social Issues, Boulder,
Colorado

TERESA D. LaFROMBOISE, Stanford University

MICHAEL LEVINE, Carnegie Corporation of New York

GERALDINE P. MANNION, Carnegie Corporation of New York

ALFRED L. McALISTER, University of Texas, Austin

HOWARD L. PINDERHUGHES, University of California,
San Francisco

LINDA POWELL, Columbia University

AVERY RUSSELL, Carnegie Corporation of New York

EDWARD SEIDMAN, New York University

ROBERT L. SELMAN, Harvard University

Preface

On November 9-10, 1998, the Forum on Adolescence of the Board on Children, Youth, and Families, a cross-cutting initiative of the Institute of Medicine and the National Research Council of the National Academy of Sciences, convened a workshop entitled Research to Improve Intergroup Relations Among Youth. Held at the request of the Carnegie Corporation of New York, this workshop considered selected findings of 16 research projects that have focused on intergroup relations among children and adolescents; all 16 received funding from Carnegie Corporation of New York for their work on this issue. The funding of these projects was part of a larger research initiative supported by Carnegie Corporation of New York that sought to update and expand the knowledge, sources, and dynamics of racial and ethnic prejudice among youth, identifying approaches to foster intergroup understanding.

The goal of the workshop was to provide an opportunity to learn about the work and preliminary findings of the 16 projects, as well as to review the knowledge base regarding the effectiveness of interventions designed to promote peaceful, respectful relations among youth of different ethnic groups.

Although the workshop on which this summary is based could provide only a glimpse of the large body of research covered by the many disciplines studying intergroup relations, it reflects the overarching mission of the Forum on Adolescence. The forum was established under the auspices of the Board of Children, Youth, and Families in 1997 to review and establish the science base regarding adolescent health and development and efforts to foster this development; identify new directions and support for research in this area, approaching research as a resource to be developed cumulatively over time; highlight new research, programs, and policies that have demonstrated promise in improving the health and well-being of adolescents; convene and foster collaboration among individuals who represent diverse viewpoints and backgrounds, with a view to enhancing the quality of leadership in this area; and disseminate research on adolescence and its policy implications to a wide array of audiences, ranging from the scientific community to the lay public.

We offer our appreciation to all of the presenters and participants for their time and contributions. Special thanks go to the Carnegie Corporation of New York staff, in particular Anthony W. Jackson, Michael Levine, Roz Rosenberg, Susan Smith, and Vivien Stewart, for their assistance and support. Thanks are also due to Zodie Makonnen and Amy Gawad of the National Research Council staff, who helped to organize the workshop, and Sandee Brawarsky, who distilled the major themes that emerged from the workshop in this summary report.

This report has been reviewed in draft form by individuals chosen for their diverse perspectives and technical expertise, in accordance with procedures approved by the National Research Council's Report Review Committee. The purpose of this independent review is to provide candid and critical comments that will assist the institution in making the published report as sound as possible and to ensure that the report meets institutional standards for objectivity, evidence, and responsiveness to the study charge. The review comments and draft manuscript remain confidential to protect the integrity of the deliberative process.

We wish to thank the following individuals for their participation in the review of this report: James A. Banks, Center for Multicultural Education, University of Washington, Seattle; Sarah Brown, National Campaign to Prevent Teenage Pregnancy, Washington, D.C.; Maxine Hayes, Community and Family Health, Washington State Department of Health; Janet W. Schofield, Learning Research and Development Center, University of Pittsburgh; and Deborah Stipek, Graduate School of Education, University of California, Los Angeles. Although the individuals listed above have provided constructive comments and suggestions, it must be emphasized that responsibility for this final report rests entirely with the authoring body and the institution.

We hope this report will stimulate and encourage those interested in fostering and promoting positive intergroup relations among youth.

David Hamburg, *Chair*
Michele D. Kipke, *Director*
Forum on Adolescence

Contents

IMPROVING INTERGROUP RELATIONS
AMONG YOUTH

Improving Intergroup Relations
Among Youth

As many times as it has been said, it is no less true: the future of America lies with its young people. It is essential to give them every opportunity to excel, to dream and realize those dreams, and to live full and healthy lives, enriched with stable and meaningful relationships. A particular challenge is to prepare them for an increasingly diverse society and to build a tradition of tolerance, acceptance, and respect for others.

Forty years after the beginning of the civil rights movement, the nation continues to be divided along lines of race and ethnicity. Still far from Martin Luther King's dream of an integrated nation, we are, in many ways, "A Country of Strangers," as the title of journalist David K. Shipler's book on race in America suggests (Shipler, 1998). Prejudice still persists, whether it is expressed in words or actions that at times can range from subtle to violent. The patterns of prejudice and discrimination that persist will exact a large economic and social toll in terms of both the number of minority group members affected and the loss of their potential contribution to society (Schofield, 1995). Early in life, children learn that race is important, and it influences how they see the world and how the world sees them (Brawarsky, 1996).

The study of interethnic and interracial interactions and relationships among youth, also called intergroup relations, has become a critical, complex, and challenging field in recent years. America's changing demographic profile has forced a redefinition of the dynamics of diversity. According to the Census Bureau, in 1980 whites accounted for 74 percent of all children in the United States, but the proportion has steadily decreased since and this trend is expected to continue through the year 2050. Blacks, who constituted the largest minority population prior to 1997, are now slightly outnumbered by Hispanic children (each accounting for nearly 15 percent of the total child population). By the year 2020, it is estimated that more than one in five U.S. children will be Hispanic, and the Asian American population is expected to increase from 4 to 6 percent by the year 2020 (Bureau of the Census, 1996). Immigration is also expected to fuel the growing diversity of the U.S. population during the coming decades. Moreover, an increasing percentage of the population is biracial or multiracial. With this increasing diversity, many individuals no longer neatly fit into the categories that have been traditionally used to define race and ethnicity in this country (Schofield, 1995).

It is also important to note that the total number of young people in the United States is also increasing, thus further heightening the need to find new ways to promote peaceful, respectful relations among them. For example, population estimates suggest that the number of adolescents in the United States will continue to increase during the next several decades, from nearly 36 million adolescents ages 10 to 19 in 1993, to 43 million in 2020 (Bureau of the Census, 1996).

As the nation becomes more varied in terms of the cultural, ethnic, and racial backgrounds of its citizens, this diversity is reflected in the student bodies of many public schools, where youth from a wide variety of backgrounds come together. The relationships among young people, as they interact in schools and in the community, are complex and have repercussions on many aspects of their school experiences, as well as their futures. In fact, research has shown that it is in school that children frequently have their first relatively close and extended opportunity for contact with those from different racial or ethnic backgrounds. Hence, whether hostility and stereotyping grow or diminish may be critically influenced by the particular experiences children have there.

Most Americans would agree that growing diversity in America should be accompanied by increased interaction, understanding, and the promise of building a society of greater humanity and peace. But anecdotal evidence suggests an alarming increase in adolescent hate crimes, organized hate groups, and overt expressions of racial intolerance, and many young people (and older ones as well) have come to hold negative views about people and groups from different backgrounds. It is therefore essential to study ways to reduce these negative forces, to find ways to build bridges among people that create an atmosphere of respect, and to create peaceful environments in which all young people can achieve their potential and not feel that, because of their language, skin color, or cultural background, they have any less claim on the American dream.

Although a substantial amount of research on relations among people of different backgrounds was conducted in the late 1960s and the 1970s, most of this work slowed down in the 1980s due in part to a shift in funding priorities. A large proportion of the research on intergroup relations from the 1960s and the 1970s focused exclusively on relations between whites and blacks. Although work on black-white relations is still relevant and extremely important, recent demographic changes make it equally important to understand relations among a much wider variety of groups, including those among different minority groups. As Schofield suggests, even if demographic change had not occurred, earlier research would be outdated because of the substantial shifts in racial attitudes that have occurred during the past 20 years on the part of both majority and minority group members. According to Schofield and workshop participants, the current literature needs to be updated and expanded (Schofield, 1989).

Against the background of an increasingly diverse America, as well as a rich body of research that spans decades but that largely stopped in 1980s, the Workshop on Research to Improve Intergroup Relations Among Youth convened an interdisciplinary group of researchers, representatives from federal and state governmental agencies, foundations, national and international organizations, and educators to examine early findings from 16 research projects funded by the Carnegie Corporation of New York. The lead researchers, all university-based, presented their observations, thoughts, findings, and suggestions for ongoing research. The studies differed in context and methodology, and some involved community and school-based interventions. Most of the studies were conducted in states with great diversity, including California, Colorado, Florida, Massachusetts, New York, Pennsylvania, and Texas.

Participants discussed their program experiences and research findings and the policy implications of this and related research, including areas in which additional research is needed. They were invited to touch on such questions as: What theoretical frameworks drive the development and implementation of intervention programs? What intervention strategies have been employed and how have they been evaluated? From these early findings, is it possible to distill for whom and under what conditions these interventions are more or less effective? What research and practice gaps remain? What efforts are required to promote positive intergroup relations among youth in the next decade and beyond?

Half of the 16 projects discussed at the workshop conducted research to examine the effectiveness of interventions designed to influence the existing dynamics in multicultural settings, and the other half focused on the impact of child and adolescent development, as well as institutional transitions, on intergroup relations. The studies probed not only relations among members of majority and minority groups, but also relations among members of different minority groups. Several studies emphasized interventions intended to prevent violence and interracial and interethnic conflict among youth. Most of the studies centered on ways to prevent or reduce prejudice among middle school and high school age youth, but several studies examined younger children. A description of each research project appears in Appendix A.

Vivien Stewart, chair of the Education Division of the Carnegie Corporation of New York, explained in her presentation that this subject has been a long-standing interest of the foundation. Through a grant program totaling $2.1 million, the aim of the foundation was to strengthen the knowledge base regarding intergroup relations, to generate models that might be replicated in other schools and communities, and to stimulate additional research interest as well as spark a new generation of scholarship. It was the foundation's hope that this activity would move these issues to a place of prominence on the national agenda, inspiring new federal research funding. According to Stewart, "until now, many programs have been based more on good intentions than on serious research."

In preparation for the workshop, the researchers were asked to present the following information about their project:

- the overall goal, study hypotheses, and methods used to conduct the research;
- key findings; and
- programmatic and policy implications of the work.

They were also asked to provide background papers describing their research in advance of the workshop; these materials were distributed to help facilitate discussion at the workshop.

The workshop was an effort intended to take stock of current knowledge on intergroup relations, highlighting key findings from recent research.

It was also convened to help inform the future work of a new, cross-cutting initiative of the Institute of Medicine and the National Research Council called the Forum on Adolescence. Given limitations of both time and scope, however, the workshop could not address a variety of issues that are certainly very important when considering how to improve intergroup relations among youth. For example, this group neither defined nor discussed diversity beyond ethnic/racial differences—such as differences in values, religious beliefs, sexual orientation, and ability.

It is important to note that this summary report has a number of limitations. First, it does not provide a comprehensive synthesis of the research findings of the 16 projects, nor does it provide a full discussion of either the successes or the problems of each project; the workshop considered each project very briefly, using a standard format. Workshop participants were given a general format for their presentations—they were asked to present the aims of the study, describe methods used, and report the major findings. Almost all chose to highlight their successes, rather than problems they may have encountered in implementing their projects or nonsignificant or negative findings. As a consequence, the workshop may have had an underlying bias in favor of "good news."

Second, the studies did not specifically address the duration of the changes that resulted from the interventions implemented in each project. In addition, the projects were funded as two-year projects, and most were not complete at the time of the workshop. This report therefore does not speak to the long-term changes observed or accomplished as a result of the interventions.

Third, at the time of the workshop, the projects were at various stages—some had requested extensions, some had just been completed, and some had received additional funding from other sources to continue the work. Consequently, participants did not discuss any lessons learned from the projects at the workshop, although this report includes a research agenda for the future.

Finally, this report is limited to a summary of presentations at the workshop, reflecting the views and statements of those attending, and does not provide a definitive analysis of the state of intergroup relations in America or the range and rich body of research on this important topic. It therefore does not provide a policy statement. Rather, it is a report based on research findings and related observations on the subject of intergroup relations as covered at the meeting.

THIS RICH AND GROWING DIVERSITY

President Clinton has written: "As we approach the 21st century, America is once again a nation of new promise, with the opportunity to become the world's first truly multiracial, multiethnic democracy. In as few as 50 years, there may be no majority race in our nation. This rich and growing diversity should be a source of great pride and strength as we enter the new millennium" (Council of Economic Advisers, 1998).

"Must children grow up to be hateful?" David Hamburg, chair of the workshop, chair of the Forum on Adolescence, and former president of the Carnegie Corporation of New York, asked the assembled workshop participants. "Education, through the family, schools, media, and community organizations, can be successfully turned into a force to reduce intergroup conflict. But the question is, how can we as humans develop a more constructive orientation toward those outside our own group while maintaining the values, the very considerable values, of primary group allegiance and firm identity?"

The tendency toward ethnocentrism—the belief in the superiority of one's own ethnic group—that is seen across the world is a natural orientation that seems to be rooted in the ancient past, according to Hamburg. Individuals seem to have a tendency to favor their own group and to regard their own community in a positive manner. Workshop participant Margaret Beale Spencer of the Graduate School of Education at the University of Pennsylvania pointed out a critical paradox associated with ethnocentrism: although it gets in the way of understanding among peoples of different backgrounds, some degree of ethnocentrism "seems necessary as a kind of glue to hold a particular society together." But when ethnocentrism prevents bridge building between cultures, it becomes maladaptive and destructive. "From ethnocentrism to racism can be a very short step," Spencer observed.

Gordon Allport has argued in his book "The Nature of Prejudice" that human groups tend to stay apart. Allport notes that this tendency "is adequately explained by the principles of ease, least effort, congeniality and pride in one's own culture" (Allport, 1954). Some researchers have also argued that given the reality of a multicultural U.S. population, one has to understand that group differences are indeed a reality and could potentially be a major source of strength for the society as a whole.

Although there is no clear agreement among researchers and policy makers about whether the development of friendships between individuals of different backgrounds ought to be a high priority, there's little disagreement that stereotyping and antagonism between groups are great and lasting costs to the well-being of society, and that individuals from diverse backgrounds need to be able to interact effectively with each other in their work and civic life.

As the world in which children and youth live has changed in terms of technology and increasing diversity, new knowledge has been gained with important implications for the task of improving intergroup relations. Workshop participants agreed, for example, that the assumption is simply untrue that merely bringing people into contact with each other will necessarily lead to mutual understanding and respect. The conditions under which contact occurs are important. The contexts in which interactions occur, attitudes develop, feelings are expressed are a critical influence on those attitudes and on the ensuing behavior (Schofield, 1995). The contact hypothesis, originally proposed after World War II by Gordon Allport and others, emphasizes four major variables for positive benefit: cooperative interaction, equal status among participants, individualized contact, and individualized support for the contact (Stephan and Stephan, 1996). Researchers have since added other, broader variables that influence whether contact leads to positive results: societal factors, which include the structure of society, the historical and current relations between the groups that are in contact; the cultural background of the groups involved; and personal factors, which include demographic characteristics, personality traits and prejudices, stereotypes, and other beliefs (Stephan and Stephan, 1996).

Researchers are developing fuller understandings of how intergroup relations can be manifested differently by boys and girls, by children at different developmental stages, and by members of different racial and ethnic groups; the latter can also vary according to which group is considered the majority or mainstream group in a particular setting. Researchers are also increasingly aware of what is called the "tension factor," which has several dimensions: specific behaviors that generate tension may differ according to the setting and the groups involved; the way both negative and positive attitudes are expressed may vary; and interventions that are helpful in some situations won't work in others (Schofield, 1989).

As Alex Stepick of Florida International University explained, there has been a shift in perceptions of Americanization, with many newcomers becoming assimilated as "hyphenated" Americans (for example, Haitian-American, Cuban-American) rather than simply as either American or as Hispanic. As large numbers of immigrants continue to arrive in the United

States, their assimilation is going to mirror the styles and culture of their peers with whom they have greatest contact—which may or may not reflect the mainstream white culture. For adolescents, Stepick observed, American culture quickly dominates immigrant ethnic roots and, in the face of prejudice, adolescents from immigrant families may assimilate rapidly, but not necessarily to mainstream white American ways. Rather they assimilate to ethnic American ways. As they assimilate, Stepick noted, they gain acceptance from their ethnic American peers and avoid discriminatory treatment. In what he calls "the context of their youth culture," they have earned the right to be part of the local society.

THE MEANING OF POSITIVE INTERGROUP RELATIONS

Although the term "positive intergroup relations" among youth is used frequently, there is no consensus among researchers as to its precise meaning. For example, to some, it means peaceful, nonviolent relations in school and outside, a kind of tolerance and coexistence; to others, it refers to something beyond tolerance that includes understanding and promoting genuine connections among groups. It could also be perceived to mean the ability of young people to look at one another and clearly see just the individuals before them. This perspective, also known as the "colorblind perspective," has been defined as a point of view that sees racial and ethnic group membership as irrelevant to the ways in which individuals should treat each other. Although this perspective is at times espoused as a goal in such arenas as schools, and it is consistent with a long-standing American emphasis on the importance of individuality, Schofield argues that it is not without some subtle problems (Schofield, 1998). She suggests that it can foster an atmosphere in which race is never mentioned and intergroup tensions are not recognized, creating an environment in which people who are basically well intentioned act in discriminatory ways.

In addition, community leaders may have different notions than scientists about what is meant by "getting along," and those notions may be related to the economic and political structure of the community as well as to its history. Workshop participants agreed that not only is it important for researchers, community leaders, school principals, and teachers to develop a common understanding of positive intergroup relations, but it also is essential to hear from young people in particular about how they understand and experience race, ethnicity, culture, and general race relations. There was considerable discussion at the workshop regarding the importance of having a clear definition of what it is that can and should be improved, as well as an idea of what an improvement might look like. Without such agreement, it is hard for all interested parties to have a meaningful discussion about issues related to the design and measurement of programs intended to improve intergroup relations.

Workshop participants agreed that there is often a disconnect between the concerns of youth and adult perceptions of their concerns; adults sometimes misread situations of conflict between youth. As Stepick noted, for young people, most conflicts with their peers are about issues of friendship and perceived betrayal, relationships, and cliques; young people worry mainly about what other young people think of them and about being accepted. Adults, for their part, may worry about the consequences of young people's behavior with respect to their future productivity. In multiracial, multiethnic settings, conflicts may appear to be about intergroup differences, but they are often about issues among friends. It is also important to point out, however, that issues that surface among friends who happen to come from different backgrounds can also be perceived by others, and even eventually by themselves, as being racially or ethnically motivated.

It is also not clear how intergroup relations relate to academic achievement and other developmental outcomes. The very phrase "academic achievement" has several meanings: to some students, parents, and school administrators, it may imply good grades and the motivation to go on to higher education; to others, it may mean simply staying in school. Some researchers have indicated that cooperative learning methods have had positive effects on academic achievement for students from varied ethnic and racial backgrounds in a variety of subject areas (Slavin, 1995). The positive effects were especially salient for methods that emphasized "group goals and individual accountability, in which cooperating groups are recognized based on the individual learning performances of all group members" (Slavin, 1995).

Another important point was brought up at the workshop: although positive intergroup relations may have the potential to build bridges between groups and reduce tensions, failed efforts to bring people together can have the opposite effect, intensifying tensions, heightening conflicts, and reinforcing stereotypes. For example, Stepick referred to an incident that took place after a Haitian dance performance at a football pep rally, in which the terms "boat people" and "Haitian" became epithets among students in a Miami school. Several factors subsequently contributed to improvement of the situation: the public school system took an active interest in increasing students' cultural awareness, and the population of the school shifted from a minority to a majority of Haitian students.

"We appear to experience diversity as inequality in this country," said Spencer, keynote speaker at the workshop. Numerous workshop participants also pointed out the "institutional silence" about race and racism and spoke of the urgent need to engage members of the community, school superintendents, school board members, principals, teachers, parents, and young people in meaningful discussions about the issue in a safe and open environment. Those who feel affirmed in their own identity are more likely to be respectful toward others.

YOUTH AND IDENTITY FORMATION

A complex web of factors affects the development of children's identity and racial attitudes, which encompasses both environmental influences and cognitive and psychosocial stages. For example, workshop participants noted, although children are born blind to distinctions of race, racial awareness starts as early as 3 years of age. The first influences on a child's identity formation—how the child comes to see himself or herself as a member of one or several racial, ethnic, cultural, and religious groups—occurs at home and in the context of family. Most significant at the earliest stages are parents and their values, specifically how they deal with issues of race, in deeds and in words. Also important is the community in which the child lives, and the messages the child encounters; later on, peers, teachers, school officials, and community leaders have significant influence.

Margaret Beale Spencer, who has long been involved in research on the development of racial attitudes, explained that racial awareness begins as early as age 3, with racial identity developing between the ages of 5 and 7. She observed that preschool children from most ethnic backgrounds often express preference for the majority white group and negative bias toward minority groups, even their own. For example, black preschoolers often express "white-valuing" attitudes, but at the same time maintain positive self-regard. For these same children at about age 6, their own race begins to have more relevance in terms of their identity, and they begin to express attitudes favoring their own group membership. At the same age, white children exhibit less bias, although their attitudes are more Eurocentric in nature. Spencer noted that the exceptions to this are families in which the parents are active and responsive, and incorporate into family life the learning and understanding of different cultures. She stressed that the earlier that children begin to receive positive messages about their own race, the more self-confident they will feel when confronted by racial stereotypes and biases. It's also important to expose children at a young age to "culturally pluralistic values," which Spencer defined as values encouraging positive racial attitudes about one's own group and respect toward others. These values need to be reinforced in all areas of a child's life—home, school, and community. During the early years, it is also important for parents to help their children establish self-accepting cultural values, so they are able to use their school experiences to focus on building skills and learning rather than struggling to cope with racial issues.

As further discussed by Spencer, children become more capable of perceiving and understanding stereotypes during the preadolescent years, with advancing cognitive development, physiological changes, and broadening social networks. Many young people are particularly self-conscious at this age as they feel their way in the world, and race consciousness is an additional level of growing self-awareness. Especially for minority youth, there is heightened awareness of race, biases, and their status in an ethnic minority group. Guidance and support from adults are as important at this stage as in the early childhood years. In general, young people may seem resilient, but they are actually quite vulnerable, particularly in middle adolescence; this may be especially true for adolescents from ethnic/racial minority groups. As a coping mechanism, many young people will distance themselves from what they perceive as a hostile school environment if they come up against an insensitive teacher or administrator. Since most teachers have little if any training in how developmental processes unfold for young people from different backgrounds, conflicts often ensue. In general, according to Spencer, there is more voluntary segregation as youth get older, and white children tend to exhibit more bias toward other races than do black children.

Several speakers referred to the unacknowledged privilege of European-American youth. In the context of how society thinks of race and race relations, many white youth do not give a lot of thought to the meaning of their racial group membership, but for minority youth, such thoughts can be ever-present.

Relevant to these general issues, in a study conducted at four schools in Denver, Colorado, workshop participant Phyllis A. Katz and her team of researchers at the Institute of Research on Social Issues found that racial attitudes in young children ages 6 to 9 are quite malleable, and that a variety of procedures could be used to foster more positive attitudes toward other races. They used perceptual training, which is a strategy intended to increase children's attention to within-race differences and to reduce assumptions that physical similarities or differences imply psychological differences. Another strategy is cognitive training, which is used to increase children's capacity for "sorting faces" along multiple criteria, in an effort to raise their cross-race empathy. These strategies called for short, focused tasks that did ultimately change many aspects of the children's race-related behaviors. These strategies are simple and straightforward and, according to Katz, this intervention could be modified for use in classrooms by teachers.

SCHOOLS AND THEIR INFLUENCE

As noted by several workshop participants, schools matter. It is in schools that young people learn what it means to be part of something larger than their family; for many young people, schools provide their first experiences of extended direct contact with people from backgrounds different from their own. Accordingly, one of the challenges for communities and educators is to create multicultural classrooms in which race and ethnic differences are openly discussed. Ideally, in such an environment, youth of all backgrounds would feel valued, would be encouraged to achieve academic success, and would feel comfortable discussing matters of race and ethnicity in a spirit of candor and trust. This would require, at a minimum, that teachers be well trained to listen and guide them.

School policies and practices can strongly influence intergroup relations. These include tracking, which usually offers differentiated classroom opportunities for students who demonstrate different learning styles or levels of achievement; cooperative learning projects, which can lead to the development of positive relations; extracurricular activities, such as sports and community service; specially designed multicultural curricular materials; and programs like school-wide assemblies. In addition, the overall institutional tone toward promoting intergroup relations can have an influence: some schools are rigid, and others are much more open to new ideas.

According to the contact hypothesis, which underpins much of the research done in the field of intergroup relations, several factors are necessary in order to improve intergroup relations through direct contact with people from different ethnic and racial backgrounds. As mentioned earlier, four factors have been put forth: the interaction must be on a level of equal status; the activities involved must be cooperative rather than competitive, leading to the achievement of common goals; there must be individualized contact among members of the group; and it must be sanctioned and supported by the institution and by authority figures within the institution. It is important for schools to create these opportunities, which form the starting point for positive intergroup interaction.

On the basis of his research in Miami, Stepick observed that although the main tenets of the contact hypothesis are valid, most schools do not fulfill its qualifications; still, they can strive toward it. He believes that racism cannot be ignored, and trying to ignore it only makes it worse. Rather, he calls on educators to affirm all students' identities and also to recognize the fact that racism does exist and, unchecked, can be divisive. Schools need not choose between having multicultural events, like special celebrations for ethnic holidays, and American cultural events, such as programs for national holidays; they can and should do both. These special activities must be more than "symbolic shadows reluctantly performed" and must be followed up by other activities requiring young people's cooperation. And the activities have to be authentic, as children will recognize anything less than that for what it is.

Hanh Cao Yu of the Social Policy Research Institute discussed her research, which was conducted in six diverse secondary schools in the state of California. She emphasized the importance of schools acknowledging group differences, observing that black students were more often the targets of inconsistent tracking, low ability grouping, disciplinary policies, and general societal discrimination. Strategies she found to be particularly effective at encouraging young people to navigate the different worlds encompassed by their families, peer groups, and school worlds—what Yu refers to as "crossing borders"—include participating in classrooms with a diverse student representation, participating in extracurricular activities in school and in the community, and developing a positive ethnic identity through family. For some students, developing a dual identity—perhaps one identity in school and a different version in the neighborhood—was an effective way to move through different worlds. She spoke of the importance of schools in creating "safe spaces" for young people to explore their feelings and building supportive friendships.

Most of the schools observed by Yu were not passive toward their increasingly diverse student bodies. She and her associates found that school principals, teachers, parents, and students were beginning to be proactive and to challenge traditional policies and practices that could lead to inequitable treatment. Yu and her colleagues also noted that there is no single path or strategy for schools to follow to promote positive intergroup relations. Every program that was attempting to improve intergroup relations among young people, in every school, must take into account students' varying needs and levels of readiness to grapple with tough issues.

In a Southern California study headed by Michele Foster of Claremont Graduate University, a sharp contrast emerged among elementary schools in a single district as to how the schools handled intergroup relations among young people from diverse backgrounds, in terms of both the tone set in the schools and classroom activities. Foster found differences between schools that "do diversity," that is, although they talk about it and hold programs and celebrations, it is not part of the real texture of the school, and those schools that truly embrace diversity, as evidenced by the varied backgrounds of the teaching staff, the number of languages spoken by the staff, and the spirit of respect among groups that seems quite natural. Schools need to do more than showcase multiculturalism. They need to live it in some authentic way beyond the superficial, Foster observed.

The study involved two districts in adjacent towns. Foster found that in both districts, there was more intergroup interaction among boys than girls, and intergroup relations decreased for girls as they got older. One reason is that the boys tended to bond through sports, roughhousing, and teasing each other. Girls, who were less interested in these types of activities, would make friends and bond through nonphysical activities, for example, playing with each other's hair and sharing clothing—things they were more comfortable doing with children from their own group. There were also differences in terms of discipline in the two districts. In the more affluent district, the black students were more likely to be considered discipline problems. At the other schools, where children were encouraged to work together, they and the teachers were more likely to look beyond race.

Fernando I. Soriano of San Diego State University conducted a study in Northern California examining the relationship between psychosocial and cultural factors as potential mediators of intercultural conflict among a diverse group of high-risk adolescent boys on probation in court schools. The study found a clear relationship between cultural factors like ethnic identity and acculturation, on one hand, and intercultural group attitudes and behavior such as violence, on the other. According to his research, both negative intercultural group attitudes and self-reported behaviors are inversely related to ethnic identity and bicultural self-efficacy. For example, as ethnic pride and identity rise, the likelihood of a youth's being a violent offender diminishes. Although there were only a small number of participants in this research, Soriano's results suggest that the interventions developed through this study may be effective in reducing intergroup conflict and preventing violence and aggression. He suggested the need for interventions that have several components.

Finally, workshop participants emphasized the fact that schools need leaders. They discussed the tendency for interventions to work best when school officials were supportive and when teachers integrated these types of interventions into the curriculum. In addition, workshop participants emphasized the need to build relationships between researchers and teachers.

THE POWER OF TEACHERS

Teachers have a profound impact on the lives of young people; their influence can be both positive and negative. They are role models, pathfinders, arbitrators, peacemakers, interpreters, mentors, promoters of civic ethics, and administrators. In addition, they're responsible for imparting skills, facts, the love of learning. Through their teaching and through their own behavior, they can be the ones who show students respect for ideas and for ways of being different. The best teachers recognize that they themselves are also students, learning from the young people they're teaching.

Workshop participants noted that teachers receive little if any guidance or professional training in how to deal with issues related to the diversity of their students; they have no preparation for facilitating in-depth discussions on race and ethnicity, nor do they learn how to deal with race-related conflicts or how to prepare young people for life in a multiracial society. In fact, many teachers are hesitant to talk about sensitive topics such as race, assuming that conversation will create tensions rather than dispel or avert them. Workshop participants stressed that teachers need advanced training in dealing with students who differ from one another, both culturally and developmentally; they also need antiracist multicultural teaching materials and advice on using them. Learning to promote positive intergroup interaction should be part of every teacher's training.

Studies have shown that teacher training in multicultural education can have a positive impact on teachers' ability to work and interact effectively with ethnically diverse student populations (Stephan, 1999). As part of their study in western Massachusetts, Beverly Daniel Tatum of Mount Holyoke College and Phyllis C. Brown of Lesley College designed a semester-long course for area teachers entitled "Effective Anti-Racist Classroom

Practices for All Students," in which participants examined their own sense of ethnic and racial identity and their attitudes toward other groups. The researchers presumed that teachers should have a strong sense of their own core identity and be able to engage in ethnic-related discussions with their peers in order to support the positive development of their students' ethnic and racial identities. Among the participating teachers, the research team found shifts in racial awareness and sense of racial identity as well as changes in classroom practice. When teachers are more comfortable talking about racial identity in any context, they respond better to the academic needs of a diverse group. Tatum's course included discussions of what she refers to as "foundational concepts," which include prejudice, racism, internalized oppression, and the distinction between passive and active racism. Tatum underlined the importance of increasing teachers' understanding of the student's background, training teachers in effectively discussing issues such as racism and stereotyping, and helping teachers to have high expectations for students of color, including academic achievement.

In her study in California, Michele Foster also found that teachers need assistance in learning to interact positively with parents from a variety of backgrounds. Teachers need to be able to deal with students and parents from all backgrounds and to understand the many dimensions of their racial, ethnic, and cultural identities. And they need to be able to use those backgrounds as resources rather than as explanations for bad behavior.

CURRICULA AS TOOLS

Whether mandated by the state or initiated by the community or the school, developed by professionals, or improvised by the classroom teacher, the curriculum can be a powerful resource in promoting positive intergroup relations; it often provides a systematic approach to helping young people understand, respect, and embrace diversity.

One study showed the potential impact of a challenging curriculum. A research team in Massachusetts led by Dennis J. Barr designed a two-part study using an innovative educational program, "Facing History and Ourselves," the aim of which is to promote the development of a more humane and informed citizenry. In the course of their involvement, 8th grade students struggled together as they studied human behavior in the light of the Holocaust and other examples of racism and oppression, drawing connections between their own lives and the breakdown of democracy and ensuing genocide. The results suggest that participating students were influenced by the program positively: they became less racist in attitude, less insular about their ethnic identity, and more aware of their responsibility toward each other and also of their own biases. In comparison to nonparticipating students, they showed increases in what Barr refers to as "relationship maturity," which encompasses increased interpersonal understanding, hypothetical and real-life interpersonal negotiation skills, and more importantly increases in their capacity to reflect on the personal meaning of relationships. The students highlighted the importance of inclusion and belonging and avoiding social isolation and victimization.

In his study probing the nature of prejudice, Ronald G. Slaby of the Education Development Center used "the bystander approach"—i.e., placing middle school students in the third-party role of bystanders to acts of prejudice, rather than in the role of perpetrator or victim. It is an educational strategy, using video as a springboard for discussion, to help people feel comfortable and to begin to understand the other's perspective. Slaby noted that the bystander perspective offers such opportunities as allowing students, from a bystander perspective, to respond to acts of prejudice as equals and without implicit or explicit blame and to view issues of prejudice more objectively, critically, and nondefensively.

SCHOOL-BASED EXTRACURRICULAR ACTIVITIES

Often it is outside the classroom walls that some of the most meaningful intergroup interactions occur. School-based extracurricular activities, like clubs and sports groups, can offer safe, meaningful places for young people to find common ground and make friends across racial and ethnic boundaries, by working or playing together in pursuit of common goals. Researchers have suggested that extracurricular activities provide an important social milieu for cooperation by providing each person with an opportunity to make a contribution that will benefit the whole (Schofield, 1995).

One study conducted in Houston used methods proven successful in preventive medicine and public health to change dangerous attitudes and, ultimately, behavior. The project sought to positively influence students' attitudes regarding intergroup relations and reduce intergroup hostility by encouraging them to write and distribute stories through the school newsletter. The stories related to increased tolerance of diversity among the students. In schools with a history of race riots and racial violence, the University of Texas researchers, led by Alfred L. McAlister, found reductions in hostile actions and in victimization through exposure to this kind of behavioral journalism. McAlister emphasized that in large, diverse communities, efficient communication methods used to influence health behavior can have positive results (see Appendix A for complete project description).

Sports teams provide opportunities for young people from different backgrounds to get to know each other in important ways as fellow team members. As suggested by Patricia Marks Greenfield, lead researcher on a University of California based study of whether sports teams promote racial tolerance and intergroup relations, sports teams have the potential to meet the criteria of equal status contact between majority and minority groups. However, the findings of her study indicate that "sports are not the panacea for intergroup relations that might have been imagined." Although teams provide opportunities for equal status—and form a natural laboratory for studying intergroup relations in multiethnic settings—they are not a guarantee of peaceful interaction between members of different racial and ethnic groups.

The most important determining factor was the coach—how he or she led the team and the values he or she stood for. The coach's leadership style is an important factor in determining how the team will operate with regard to racial and ethnic differences—whether it functions as a unified group, as a team with a racial hierarchy, or one with a split across racial lines. Also important were the internal dynamics of the team, whether the coach and players emphasized individualistic or collective values, and whether they encouraged or accepted players' self-enhancement or modesty. Among the things that can promote harmony on a multiethnic team are ensuring that the coach treats all members equally and responds to conflict as a group problem in a public manner.

PEER INFLUENCE

Several of the studies presented at the workshop looked at the role of peers in promoting positive intergroup relations. Peer preference, as well as peer influence, involves such factors as who young people hang out with on the playground and sit with in class, which clubs they join, how they view "border crossing," and whether they have cross-race friendships and integrated social networks. Children often follow the lead of other children. Their contact with other young people can powerfully affect their skills and abilities to live in a racially and ethnically diverse world.

In a study conducted with elementary school students in an integrated district near New York City, Diane Hughes of New York University looked at the factors underlying homogeneous peer groups, more specifically, the social and developmental factors related to intergroup relations during middle childhood. As children get older, their sense of self as a member of an ethnic or racial group becomes increasingly salient, and they become more oriented toward their own group. The study had three major findings: white students were more likely to report same-race friendships than black students at any particular time; the shift toward friendships with children of the same race occurred more frequently for white students than for black students; and at any point in time, there is much variation in the children's own reports of same- and different-race friends. Black girls were more likely than black boys to report same-race friendships; Hughes explained that it may be related to boys' greater involvement in sports teams. When children reported feeling more positive toward their own group, they were more likely to associate with same-race peers. And the more they perceived that they were treated unfairly because of racial issues, the more they stayed with friends from their own group.

Looking at two contrasting ethnically diverse middle schools in Texas, Cindy Carlson of the University of Texas, Austin, led a team of researchers in a multimethod study of peer relationship patterns. They found that intergroup relationships improved across the early adolescent years. In particular, the study directed attention to the nature of borders, which arise when certain knowledge, skills, and behavior in one world are more highly valued and rewarded than in another. Of particular importance in determining to what degree students will cross borders is the school environment.

Young people are highly influenced by the attitudes of their peers, both their close friends and the members of the larger cliques or groups they belong to. In the Texas study, ethnic differences played a role: minority youth expressed less openness to diversity than their nonminority counterparts, and non-Hispanic youth had the fewest cross-race best friendships. In this study, having a positive view of one's self and one's own group correlated with having a more positive view of other groups, regardless of ethnicity. The study suggests that interventions should consider the importance of the role of peers in influencing intergroup attitudes; it also suggests the potential importance of peer groups and interventions strongly directed toward group self-esteem. Carlson cautioned that schools need to pay serious attention to whatever group is in the minority.

In an ethnographic study of a school-based program in Buffalo, New

York, Lois Weis of the State University of New York, Buffalo, found that young women, through open discussion on a variety of subjects of shared interest, developed friendships across ethnic and racial borders. Facilitated by professionals in a small group setting, the program, called "My Bottom Line," was attended voluntarily by teenagers in a magnet arts academy in the public school system; the program's goal was to "prevent or delay the onset of sexual activity, build self-esteem and increase self-sufficiency in young women through an abstinence-based, gender specific education program." The diverse group of participants used the program to refashion their identities, talking about race, femininity, teenage social issues, sexuality, stereotyping, and other topics, challenging each other and themselves in a safe atmosphere. This study was part of a larger project involving interracial communities, with integrated spaces for youth to interact, in three settings. Weis explained that each setting offered program participants an environment in which differences were acknowledged and respected and interracial relations could grow and be nourished. The researchers stressed that they created settings in which "youth could come together intellectually, aethestically and politically."

Howard L. Pinderhughes of the University of California, San Francisco, conducted both an intervention and a research project that included survey and qualitative research in a racially diverse high school in San Francisco. At Mission High School, intergroup relations were characterized by coexistence with little tension but a general lack of knowledge about others. Separate communities existed, in other words, organized by racial and ethnic group, language, and immigrant status.

The aim of the project was both to study the state of intergroup relations and to develop an action plan for building closer relations in the school. The intervention involved the creation of the P.R.O.P.S. (People Respecting Other People) program, in which students from a variety of backgrounds were recruited to join; they then conducted survey research and interviews, working both to increase the student body's awareness of their school's ethnic and racial attitudes and relations and to enhance the school's multicultural climate.

Results of the survey indicated that the most tolerant groups of students in the school were young people of mixed racial or ethnic background and Pacific Islander youth. Immigrant youth had more intolerant attitudes than members of their ethnic group who had been in the United States longer. As reported by the researchers, because of changes in the school administration, action plans intended to set the stage for the development of programs and curricula to enhance cross-cultural awareness and interaction have yet to be instituted. However, the researchers and the young people believe that youth-driven programs have great potential for having a positive impact on intergroup relations. This project underscored the simple idea that young people can be useful resources for improving intergroup relations among their peers.

AT HOME: PARENTS AND THEIR INFLUENCE

Workshop participants agreed that parents are their children's first teachers about intergroup relations. It is at home where young people get their primary information, both implicitly and explicitly, about their own racial and ethnic identity, and where they pick up attitudes about other groups. (Workshop participants also noted parenthetically that sometimes, as young people grow up, the tables may turn and children may teach their parents.) In her New York University study of elementary school students, Hughes confirmed that parents' messages about race are extremely important to the children's developing sense of identity. She found that parents' reports about their own same- and other-race friendships were very important to black youth, less so for white youth.

Tatum's Massachusetts study also included components involving students, teachers, and parents. Parents of middle school students attended a series of meetings to discuss issues related to adolescent identity development and intergroup relations in the school. Through the meetings, parents were encouraged to explore and improve their own intergroup relations as a way of modeling behavior for the students, and some parents served as resources in other components of the program. The researchers found that the parents, as well as the teachers and the youth, benefited from having settings to explore personal attitudes and to reflect on their own and others' attitudes about intergroup relations.

IN THE COMMUNITY

As discussed at the workshop, the community shapes what goes on in the schools in many ways. Constance Flanagan of Pennsylvania State University examined some of the larger issues surrounding intergroup relations, posing the question of what binds Americans together as a people. In her presentation, she quoted President Jimmy Carter's farewell address in 1981: "America did not invent human rights. In a very real way, it's the other way around. Human rights invented America. Ours was the first nation in the history of the world to be founded explicitly on such an idea." Flanagan's study examined young people's perceptions about justice, opportunity, politics, and the responsibilities of citizenship and how their outlook is influenced by the messages sent to them by communities, schools, teachers, and parents.

Through focus groups and surveys of adolescents in four communities in Pennsylvania and Michigan, three urban and one rural, Flanagan and her team found that young people learn a great deal at home about other people's rights, responsibility to others, anger and disrespect to others, values, how the self is linked with notions of public good, and public awareness about prejudice. Students who reported that they have experienced prejudice, or that someone close to them has, are less likely to believe that America is a just society. Their personal experiences are as important as are school and community influences. Young people who felt that their teachers were fair and would intervene in acts of intolerance were more likely to think of America as a just society. In addition, if they felt that the police in their community were fair, they were more likely to think of America as a just society. Although it is unclear in this case whether correlation translates into causation, according to Flanagan, doing community service, which she suggests may correlate positively with a desire to promote intergroup understanding, should be part of children's education. She also cautions against policy directions toward privatizing public education if such efforts further homogenize young people's experience.

THE ROLE OF MEDIA AND TECHNOLOGY

Workshop participants agreed that media can play an important role in a democratic society by providing accurate information so that citizens can make informed decisions. Ruby Takanishi, in her presentation at the workshop, emphasized the myriad changes in the world of technology and the media and the potential positive influence they can have in terms of interpersonal values, behaviors, and relationships over time.

Flanagan's research suggests that opportunities provided by the media that enable young people and adults to discuss current events can help youth see the connections between their own lives and the larger world and may promote intergroup tolerance. Furthermore, Flanagan's work also suggests that some young people are aware of how the media sometimes use stereotypes, presenting certain peoples and ethnic groups in stereotypically negative ways, and that they would benefit from opportunities at home and in school to discuss these images.

In the classroom, media can be effective in promoting positive interactions. In an intervention-based research project, Sherryl Browne Graves of Hunter College introduced a video series on prejudice reduction, called "Different and the Same," to elementary school students as a way to examine how media can be used in the classroom to influence intergroup relations. She found that the video, which is based on a curriculum that emphasizes the principles of fairness, awareness, inclusion, and respect, does have an effect on children: those exposed to it were more likely to endorse strategies for promoting prejudice reduction than participants in the control group who did not view the video. The video was most effective for inspiring changes in knowledge, followed by changes in attitude; the least influenced aspect was behavior. According to Graves, in general, white children were less likely to endorse inclusive strategies, exhibit positive racial attitudes, or engage in positive intergroup interactions than other groups of children. Graves also called for the design of programs in the media with characteristics that will enhance intergroup relations.

TOWARD A NEW RESEARCH AGENDA: THE CHALLENGES

Many of the studies presented at the workshop raised as many questions as answers. Workshop participants agreed that much research is still necessary to gain competence in promoting respectful and peaceful intergroup relations among young people. Workshop participants noted the need for longitudinal studies of intergroup and ethnic relations over the life span, to follow children as they grow into adolescence and beyond. In addition, participants discussed the need to engage a broader range of disciplines than those represented at the workshop. Specifically, participants noted that it would be useful to involve viewpoints from the fields of political science, public policy, law, religion, architecture, journalism, and urban affairs, for example, to probe the effects of housing policies on intergroup relations, how the design of school buildings influences the institutional climate, how the economies of communities are affected by diversity, and how to eliminate poverty for all children. And cross-national studies are also important, looking beyond the United States in order to study democracies with lessons to impart about building and maintaining positive intergroup relations. It is also possible that other institutions that place a premium on peaceful, respectful human relations, such as faith communities, may have strategies worth studying.

The studies reviewed at the workshop also raise questions as to what generalizations can be drawn from specific findings, how to disentangle associations from causality, how results can be duplicated in other settings, and how successful interventions or best practices can be reproduced on a larger scale. New and creative evaluation methodologies are essential. In thinking about future research and related strategies and policy, it is crucial to hear the voices of young people themselves about how they are experiencing and managing intergroup relations. Their encounters, their opinions, and their hopes should be considered in planning for the future.

It is not only children who need to be educated, coaxed, and guided in this area. Adults also need to look with full candor into their own attitudes and belief systems. Along with parents, family members, teachers, school officials, and other adults also have influence on young people, through their public behavior and the messages they project; politicians, as well as people in the media and the arts, need to be educated and sensitized to these issues and their responsibilities to young people.

Sometimes the lines among scholarship, research, practice, advocacy, and policy making can be fine ones. Many of the researchers at the workshop spoke of the need for bridge building in these key areas, in order to translate work in one area into strategies for change in another. Kenyon Chan, dean of the College of Liberal Arts at Loyola Marymount University, suggested that researchers have a responsibility to help teachers and other practitioners implement new methods and ideas. "We have an obligation when we do this research to make sure it is translated by us to practitioners in very practical terms," he said.

Chan also observed that these interventions are relatively small in scale, and that one major racist act in a school has the potential to wipe out positive effects. He called for attacking the challenges of intergroup relations on a broad "ecological" basis, involving the media, schools, parents, grandparents, and others, as well as the political leadership. Many of the researchers and others present echoed his sense of urgency and the need for a systemic approach to putting changes in place to improve the quality of intergroup relations in an enduring way.

References and Bibliography

Allport, G.W.
    1954   *The Nature of Prejudice.* Boston: Beacon Press.

Braddock, J.H., M.P. Dawkins, and G.Wilson
    1995   Intercultural contact and race relations among youth. In *Toward a Common Destiny: Improving Race Relations in America,* W.D. Hawley and A.W. Jackson, eds. San Francisco: Jossey-Bass Publishers.

Brawarsky, S.
    1996   *Improving Intergroup Relations Among Youth.* New York: Carnegie Corporation of New York

Bureau of the Census
    1965   Estimates of the population of the United States by single years of age, color, and sex: 1900 to 1959. *Current Population Reports,* Series P-25, No. 311. Washington, D.C. : U.S. Department of Commerce

    1974   Estimates of the population of the United States by age, sex, and race: April 1, 1960 to July 1, 1973. *Current Population Reports,* Series P-25, No. 519. Washington, D.C. : U.S. Department of Commerce.

    1982   Preliminary estimates of the population of the United States by age, sex, and race: 1970 to 1981. *Current Population Reports,* Series P-25, No. 917. Washington, D.C. : U.S. Department of Commerce.

    1996   Population projections of the United States by age, sex, and race and Hispanic origin: 1995 to 2050. *Current Population Reports,* Series P-25, No. 1130. Washington, D.C. : U.S. Department of Commerce.

    1999   Unpublished estimate tables for 1980 to 1997: Bureau of the Census Web Site. Available electronically: www.census.gov.

Council of Economic Advisers
1998   Foreword by President William Jefferson Clinton in *Changing America: Indicators of Social and Economic Well-Being by Race and Hispanic Origin.* Prepared for the President's Initiative on Race (September). Washington, D.C.: Council of Economic Advisers.
Du Bois, W.E.B.
1903   *The Souls of Black Folk: Essays and Sketches.* Chicago: A.C. McClurg & Co.
Dovidio, J.F., and S.L.Gaertner, eds.
1986   *Prejudice, Discrimination, and Racism.* Orlando, FL: Academic Press.
Garcia, E.E., and A. Hurtado
1995   Becoming American: A review of current research on the development of racial and ethnic identity in children. In *Toward a Common Destiny: Improving Race Relations in America,* W.D. Hawley and A.W. Jackson, eds. San Francisco: Jossey-Bass Publishers.
Hawley, W.D.
1995   Our unfinished task. In *Toward a Common Destiny: Improving Race Relations in America,* W.D. Hawley and A.W. Jackson, eds. San Francisco: Jossey-Bass Publishers.
Hawley, W.D., and A.W. Jackson, eds.
1995   *Toward a Common Destiny: Improving Race Relations in America.* San Francisco: Jossey-Bass Publishers.
National Research Council
1989   *Common Destiny: Blacks and American Society.* Committee on the Status of Black Americans, National Research Council. Washington, D.C.: National Academy Press.
Schofield, J.
1997   Improving race and ethnic relations among America's youth. In *Education and the Development of American Youth.* The Aspen Institute, Fifth Conference 13(1).
1998   Research on Improving Intergroup Relations Among Youth: Where Does It Stand and Where Should It Head? Presentation at planning meeting on Respect for Diversity: Race and Ethnic Relations Among Youth, November 11. Forum on Adolescence, Washington, DC.
1995   Promoting positive intergroup relations in school settings. In *Toward a Common Destiny: Improving Race Relations in America,* W.D. Hawley and A.W. Jackson, eds. San Francisco: Jossey-Bass Publishers.
1989   *Black and White in School: Trust, Tension, or Tolerance?* New York: Teachers College, Columbia University.
Shipler, D.K.
1998   *A Country of Strangers: Blacks and Whites in America.* New York: Random House.
Slavin, R.E.
1995   Enhancing intergroup relations in schools: Cooperative learning and other strategies. In *Toward a Common Destiny: Improving Race Relations in America,* W.D. Hawley and A.W. Jackson, eds. San Francisco: Jossey-Bass Publishers.

Smith, T.W.

   1998   Intergroup relations in contemporary America: An overview of survey research. In *Intergroup Relations in the United States: Research Perspectives*, W. Winborne and R. Cohen, eds. Bloomsburg, PA: Haddon Craftsmen.

Stephan, W.G.

   1999   *Reducing Prejudice and Stereotyping in Schools.* New York: Teacher's College, Columbia University.

Stephan, W.G., and W.S. Stephan

   1996   Intergroup Relations. J. Harvey, ed. Boulder, CO: Westview Press.

Winborne, W., and R. Cohen

   1998   Racial inequality and race relations issues in selected public policy areas. In *Intergroup Relations in the United States: Research Perspectives*, W. Winborne and R. Cohen, eds. Bloomsburg, PA: Haddon Craftsmen.

Appendixes

APPENDIX
A

Project Descriptions

The Workshop on Research to Improve Intergroup Relations Among Youth highlighted the findings of 16 research projects on intergroup relations among youth, each of which received initial funding from the Carnegie Corporation of New York in 1996, as part of its research initiative on race and ethnic relations. This appendix, drawn from the principal investigators' own materials, describes each project in more detail.

Project Title: Improving Interpersonal and Intergroup Relations Among Youth: A Study of the Processes and Outcomes of Facing History and Ourselves

Principal Investigator: Dennis J. Barr

Purpose: The research examines intergroup relations among youth in the context of an educational program, Facing History and Ourselves (FHAO), that seeks to promote the development of a more humane and informed citizenry. The two overarching aims of the research were accomplished in two interrelated studies: (a) an outcome study to evaluate whether a classroom-based model of FHAO promotes growth in psychosocial competencies (interpersonal understanding, interpersonal skills, and personal meaning) moral and ethnic identity development, increases in positive civic attitudes and participation, and reductions in fighting behavior and attitudes about racism, and (b) a qualitative case study of an FHAO classroom to gain basic knowledge regarding the development of psychosocial competencies that underlie interpersonal development and intergroup relations. Both studies shared the goal of adapting an existing developmental model for research on intergroup relations.

Methodology: The evaluation/outcome study used a quasi-experimental design involving 409 8th grade students and 9 teachers in 14 FHAO and 8 comparison sections. FHAO units were 10 weeks in duration. Questionnaires and a newly developed writing exercise were administered pre-test (fall) and post-test (spring). One diverse 8th grade FHAO classroom in a transitional urban/suburban neighborhood was chosen for the intensive qualitative case study of students engaging with FHAO and issues of intergroup relations in their own lives. Field notes were taken and pre- and post-interviews with students and the teacher were conducted by a participant-observer.

Key/Major Findings: The outcome study demonstrates the efficacy of the FHAO program in promoting interpersonal and intergroup relations. FHAO students showed increased relationship maturity and decreased fighting behavior, racist attitudes, and insular ethnic identity relative to comparison students. The study highlights the benefits of using a developmental measure of psychosocial competencies to evaluate developmental character education programs that are based on similar assumptions.

The qualitative case study revealed critical incidents in the students' peer culture, which highlight the importance to early adolescents of inclusion and belonging and avoiding social isolation and victimization. In one incident, breaches of trust in an ethnically diverse, popular girls' group resulted in the ostracism of one of the members. In another incident, a racist remark by an Eastern-European immigrant girl reinforced her low social status and led to intensified social and even physical victimization. These controversial incidents and dynamics within their peer groups were, in many cases, the key points of reference for students as they made sense of the central themes of their FHAO course. Abstract conceptions such as the roles played by bystander, victim, perpetrator, and resister in history, for example, came to life for individual students as they struggled to make sense of and respond to personal and often painful experiences in their peer relationships.

Programmatic/Policy Implications: Both the outcome study and the case study demonstrate that 8th graders are most meaningfully engaged with issues of social justice within their own peer society, suggesting the importance of teaching strategies that encourage connecting FHAO course themes to critical incidents in the students' peer culture that many students are aware of and concerned about. Furthermore, variation in the psychosocial maturity reflected in the students' perspectives on the critical intergroup incidents and the connection of FHAO to such issues suggests the importance of promoting teacher awareness of, and skills in engaging, students who differ from one another, both culturally and developmentally, in relation to intergroup issues raised by the course. This research underscores the value of programs that encourage young people to grapple with the connections between a historical case study of the breakdown of democracy and genocide and their own lives as a means of promoting their active and mature involvement in relation to intergroup issues and problems in their lives. Research on teacher professional development activities, such as those conducted by FHAO, is needed in order to identify those practices most likely to promote the awareness and skills teachers need to sensitively and competently integrate controversial and personally meaningful material within their classrooms.

Contact:

Dennis J. Barr
63 Norfolk Street
Cambridge, MA 02139
617-232-8390 x2203
Email: reedbarr@aol.com

Terry Tollefson
Facing History and Ourselves
16 Hurd Road
Brookline, MA 02146-6919
617-735-1630

Project Title: Intergroup Relations Among Middle School Youth

Principal Investigators: Cindy Carlson and Laura Lein

Purpose: Strengthen our knowledge base of intergroup peer relationship patterns during early adolescence.

Methodology: A comprehensive ecological survey was completed by all students in attendance at two public, ethnically diverse middle schools. In addition to the student survey, ethnographic observations were conducted within the school settings and focus groups were conducted with selected groups of students.

Key/Major Findings:
1. Intergroup attitudes steadily improved across the early adolescent years.
2. School environment influences many aspects of intergroup relations. Cross-race friendships are highly dependent upon the opportunity structure created by racial percentages. Intergroup relations varied depending upon the multicultural climate, racial balance, and use of tracking in the school.
3. Peer affiliations, both clique and crowd membership, also exert a significant influence on intergroup attitudes and behaviors.
4. Significant ethnic differences characterized intergroup attitudes with minority youth expressing less openness to diversity but non-Hispanic white youth having the fewest cross-race best friendships.
5. Regression models found that both individual and peer processes predicted intergroup attitudes.
6. Mediational models found that high self-esteem mediated the relationship between ethnic identity and openness to others, with higher self-esteem associated with more positive other group attitudes regardless of ethnicity.

Programmatic/Policy Implications:
1. Consider carefully racial balance in desegregation patterns; consider the negative impact of within-school segregation patterns created by tracking.
2. Improve multicultural climate of schools regardless of school composition.

3. Consider the important role of peers in influencing intergroup attitudes; target interventions to the peer group.
4. Individual and group interventions directed toward the development of a positive self-image may be important contributors to intergroup relations.

Contact:

Cindy Carlson
Professor
Department of Educational Psychology
University of Texas at Austin
Sanchez Building 504
Austin, TX 78712-1296
512-471-4155 x4
512-471-1288 (fax)
Email: cindy.carlson@mail.utexas.edu

Laura Lein
School of Social Work
Department of Anthropology
University of Texas at Austin
1925 San Jacinto
Austin, TX 78712-1203
512-471-9248
512-471-9514 (fax)

Project Title: Intergroup Understanding, Social Justice, and the "Social Contract" in Diverse Communities of Youth

---

Principal Investigator: Constance A. Flanagan

Purpose: This project examines adolescents' perceptions of intergroup relations as these intersect with their norms for citizenship. It examines teens' beliefs about justice and opportunity in America and the correlates of those views. We have framed the project as a study of adolescents' views of the "social contract" in America, by which we mean the sets of rights, privileges, and obligations that bind members of our society to one another. The theoretical basis for the study was drawn from the contention that Americans are fundamentally concerned about equality—but it is the form of equality and the nature of a just society that arouse debate.

Methodology: The project involved focus groups and surveys of 12 to 18-year-olds in four communities (three urban and one rural) chosen for their different demographic composition. A total of 1,119 adolescents from African (n = 115), Arab (n = 115), Puerto Rican and Dominican (n = 140), and European (n = 749) backgrounds participated.

Key/Major Findings: Although ethnic identification had no influence, personal experiences of prejudice, whether toward oneself or toward friends or loved ones, were strongly related to adolescents' beliefs that America is an unjust society. But school and community practices made a difference. Youth were more likely to believe that America is a just society if they felt their teachers were fair and would intervene in acts of student intolerance or bullying. In addition, youth were more likely to believe that America is a just society if they felt the police in their community were fair and that the community itself was a caring place. Engaging in community service was positively related to young people's desire to promote intergroup understanding and with their commitments to public interest goals. Among the "enemy images" adolescents listed as prominent in the media today were Arabs, Muslims, African-Americans, Latinos, Asians, communists, gangs, militia groups, and the American government.

Programmatic/Policy Implications: Our data point to the pivotal role of teachers in promoting a civic ethic. Choices about intervention or nonintervention in acts of intolerance send a message about the ethics of a civil society and about justice in that society. A hands-off policy that allows some youth to be ostracized or bullied sends the wrong message about the principles that bind us together as people. Opportunities to engage in service to the community should be a normative expectation of children's education; in our data, it was correlated with a desire to promote intergroup understanding and to serve the public or common good. Policy directions toward privatizing public education should be viewed with caution if they further homogenize young people's experience.

The media have an important role in a democracy—of providing accurate information so that the public can make informed choices. There are two implications regarding the media from our data: first, opportunities to discuss current events with adults can help young people see the connections of their lives with the broader society and appears to be implicated in their desire to promote intergroup understanding; second, youth are cognizant of the "enemy images" promulgated in the media and would benefit from opportunities (in school or youth groups) to deconstruct those stereotypes.

Contact:

Constance Flanagan
Associate Professor
Agricultural and Extension Education
Pennsylvania State University
University Park, PA 16802-2601
814-863-3824
814-863-4753 (fax)
Email: cflanagan@psu.edu

Project Title: A Tale of Two Towns: Intergroup Relations in Culturally Diverse Classrooms and Communities

---

Principal Investigator: Michele Foster

Purpose: To explore the effect that attending racially and ethnically mixed classrooms has on intergroup relations among children from diverse backgrounds; to describe the nature of relations between different ethnic groups, and examine the social processes that occur in ethnically diverse classrooms in order to illuminate how these processes lead to specific patterns of intergroup relations.

Methodology: We used ethnographic research methods and techniques of analysis. Systematic participant observation, qualitative interviews—informal, unstructured and semistructured, document analysis, and audiotape recording are the primary data analysis. These data have been supplemented by structured techniques, such as network analysis, designed to chart the social networks within the classroom, and sociometric measures, such as peer nomination in which students choose partners for various academic and social activities. Although the study was focused mainly at the school and classroom level, we also collected data on the macro level—institutional and community forces that affect local classroom social processes, behavior, and interaction through time—in order to understand how the historical, cultural, and sociopolitical factors influenced what we were observing in the classrooms.

Key/Major Findings: As children move into the intermediate grades (4-5), their participation in voluntary intergroup relations declines. This is more the case for girls than boys. Boys have more intergroup contact and this typically revolves around sports and banter and humor around what they consider "gross" topics. In contrast, as girls enter the intermediate grades, the grooming behavior in which they have engaged since the primary grades takes place strictly intragroup. The elite school district we observed was more self-conscious than the working-class district in its attention to organizing activities related to diversity, such as festivals, music concerts, art displays, and prejudice reduction workshops. Despite this attention, in the more elite school district, African American and Latino children were more likely to be in the lowest-achieving groups compared to Asian and Anglo children, and African American children were most likely to be perceived as discipline problems and as creating more challenges around discipline for their teachers. Teachers felt ill-equipped to deal with the tensions around discipline, with the result that African American children were overrepresented among those suspended and referred to special education. While the challenges around discipline most often concerned African American boys, African American girls also presented challenges, particularly when their teachers were male. African American pupils presented fewer discipline problems in the classrooms of African American teachers. African American parents in the elite district also expressed more dissatisfaction over their children's treatment in schools and less ability to influence the schools' decisions regarding their children.

Programmatic/Policy Implications: Schools need to go beyond superficial displays of diversity. Professional educators need professional development activities that help them (1) engage (including learning to deal with conflict) and interact productively with parents and students from all ethnic backgrounds; (2) to understand and learn how to use their students' family and cultural backgrounds as resources for engagement in the teaching/learning process rather than as excuses for student disengagement, misbehavior, and failure; (3) develop the capacity, dispositions, and instructional strategies to teach students from different ethnic backgrounds well, so that the status inequities related to academic achievement do not reinforce attitudes and exacerbate intergroup tensions; and (4) to learn how to talk about ethnicity, difference, race, racial inequity, and racism in order to help their students engage in conversations about these issues.

Contact:
Michele Foster
25 Standish Court
Crockett, CA 94525-1417
510-787-1962
Email: michelf9@idt.net

Project Title*: Different and the Same*: A Study of the Impact of a Prejudice-Reduction Video Series on Children

Principal Investigator: Sherryl Browne Graves

Purpose: Do racially and ethnically diverse children exhibit lower levels of prejudice and higher levels of positive intergroup interaction after exposure to a prejudice-reduction video series? Does the nature and amount of prejudice reduction vary with participant characteristics, including race, ethnicity, and gender? How do contextual variables, like school and classroom climate, influence the effect of the video series on children? Do any effects of the video series intervention persist beyond the immediate post-viewing period?

Methodology: The research included quasi-experimental designs in naturalistic settings of classrooms. Data was collected from classroom groupings, and therefore random assignment of subjects to intervention and nonintervention conditions was not possible. In some conditions, teachers received training on the use of the series in the classroom along with the teacher's guide; in other cases, teachers received the teacher's guide and had to prepare on their own. Children were individually administered attitudinal, behavioral, and cognitive measures before and after the video intervention. School and classroom climate was assessed in multiple ways, including interviews and classroom observations. Data was collected on how teachers presented the video series to document the context for the findings.

Key/Major Findings: *Different and the Same* had an effect on children. First, in general, children exposed to the intervention were more likely to endorse strategies for promoting prejudice reduction and positive intergroup interaction than were children in the control groups. The effect was greatest for changes in knowledge, followed by changes in attitude. The least affected dependent variable was that of behavior. In general, white children were less likely to endorse inclusive strategies, exhibit positive racial attitudes, or engage in positive intergroup interactions than were other groups of children. School and classroom contexts appear to be influential in mediating the effect of the video on particular outcome variables.

Programmatic/Policy Implications: *Different and the Same* can influence children in different ways. The nature of the effect seemed to vary along a number of dimensions. Behavior was the least affected domain, except in a case of teacher-intensive support for a particular video message. While children were generally more likely to select more diverse partners on socio-metric tasks after viewing, this greater tendency toward inclusion was not reflected in their observed behavior, which raises the question: What type of video or classroom intervention would be required to alter children's actual intergroup interactions? One area of further exploration may be in the ways in which teachers control and direct group interactions. Perhaps, the future analysis of teacher-student classroom interactions will provide additional insights in this area.

A video series designed to reduce prejudice can be effective with young children. The influence of the *Different and the Same* video series was evident in children and to a lesser extent in their teachers. A video series can affect children, but the nature of the effect varies along a number of dimensions, including interpersonal and contextual dimensions. This study also underscores the added benefits of adult mediated television and video experiences for young children. Adult mediated and extended activities seemed to enhance the influence of *Different and the Same* on children. This research suggests a need to examine teacher preparation and in-service professional development programs. It also suggests the need to examine the roles of administrative, school district, and state policies regarding the use of video and television in the classroom and the importance of the creation and maintenance of positive intergroup interaction.

Contact:
Sherryl Browne Graves
Educational Foundations and
Counseling Programs
Hunter College, CUNY
695 Park Avenue
New York, NY 10021
212-772-4710
212-772-4731 (fax)

Project Title: Fostering Positive Intergroup Attitudes in Young Children

Principal Investigator: Phyllis A. Katz

Purpose: The present study assessed the effectiveness of perceptual or cognitive training in lowering young children's (ages 6 to 9) racial biases. The current study had two primary goals: (a) to assess whether such techniques would be effective in reducing prejudice in younger children and, if so, (b) to ascertain which strategies would be most effective.

Methodology: The *perceptual training* modification strategy had two goals: (a) to increase children's attention to within-race differences and (b) to reduce assumptions that physical similarities or differences imply psychological ones. The *cognitive training* modification strategy also had two goals: (a) to increase children's capacity for sorting faces along multiple criteria and (b) to raise their level of cross-race empathy. A pre-post design was employed that utilized four measures. Two of these directly measured children's attitudes; a third assessed social distance toward same- and other-race children; a fourth interview measure assessed playmate preferences and understanding of race differences. A sample of 142 children (kindergarten through 3rd grade) was drawn from four racially integrated schools in Denver, Colorado. Half were Euro-American and half African-American. Children were randomly assigned to either of the two treatment conditions discussed above (perceptual or cognitive) or to a no-treatment control group that received the pre- and post-tests with no intervention.

Key/Major Findings: Children differed on the pre-tests, prior to the introduction of modification strategies. White children exhibited more bias than black children. These differences were more pronounced on ingroup favoritism (i.e., positive same-race associations) than on negative outgroup attributions. Age interacted with race group, revealing that black children's bias levels increased with age, whereas white children's decreased. White children also exhibited stronger preferences for same-race playmates and used racial cues more readily to judge their similarity and dissimilarity to other children.

The various treatment conditions did affect children's post-test bias levels. Effects were not always consistent across groups or measures, however. The perceptual intervention condition lowered bias levels on both attitude measures relative to the control group. It also affected playmate choices and racial constancy responses (for whites). The cognitive condition was less consistent. It lowered same-race positive attribution bias, but increased other-race negative attributions.

The findings were complex, but the perceptual training was generally associated with more consistent effects than the cognitive training employed. More fine-grained analyses of children's performance during the training sessions revealed that lower post-test bias scores for the cognitive condition were found for those who exhibited the highest cross-race empathy.

Programmatic/Policy Implications: The present findings demonstrate that the racial attitudes of young children are quite malleable and that a variety of procedures can be used effectively to foster more positive racial attitudes. Increasing perceptual differentiation and reducing children's assumptions that physical similarity is correlated with psychological characteristics resulted in lower bias levels. The modification strategies changed many other aspects of children's race-related behaviors. The relatively simple and straightforward experimental tasks employed to effect such changes could be modified so as to be incorporated by teachers in classroom situations.

Contact:
Phyllis Katz
Institute for Research on Social Problems
520 Pearl Street
Boulder, CO 80302
303-449-7782
303-449-6694 (fax)
Email: katzp@spot.colorado.edu

Project Title: Forging a Multicultural School Environment: An Examination of Intergroup Relations at an Inner-City High School— The P.R.O.P.S. Program

---

Principal Investigator: Howard Pinderhughes

Purpose: The P.R.O.P.S. Program (People Respecting Other People) was created in 1996 as an innovative project designed to improve intergroup interaction and awareness by building a multicultural community at Mission High School in San Francisco. Mission High has a racially diverse student body: 40 percent Latino, 28 percent Chinese, 16 percent Filipino, 14 percent African-American, and 2 percent white. Despite its incredible diversity, intergroup relations at Mission High School have been characterized by little interaction among groups of different ethnic backgrounds and weekly episodes of conflict and violence between groups. The project is designed to produce a clearer focus on intergroup relations within Mission High School, the development of an action plan for the adoption and development of programs and curricula to increase cross-cultural awareness and interaction, and a reduction in the level of intergroup conflict at the school. What makes the program unique is that it encourages young people themselves to lead the movement for improving intergroup relations.

Methodology: High school students are recruited and trained to conduct survey research and interviews on ethnic and racial attitudes, ethnic and racial identities, and intergroup relations among students at Mission High School. P.R.O.P.S. is also an intervention program designed to increase the school population's awareness of the current state of ethnic and racial attitudes and relations among students at the school. The survey results are presented by P.R.O.P.S. members to the school community through classroom presentations and faculty meetings as a curriculum that encourages discussions on how to improve race relations at the school. In this way, the entire student body participates in the discussion and in developing strategies for improvement. P.R.O.P.S. members will then convene working groups composed of students and faculty to develop a 3-year plan of action to enhance the multicultural environment of the school and improve intergroup relations.

Key/Major Findings: For the majority of students, intergroup relations among students at Mission High School are characterized by coexistence and limited interaction. About one-third of the students at the school cross cultural lines in their choice of friends. Contact and interaction is affected by immigrant status and language difference, which appear to function as barriers to interaction. One-quarter of students report having encountered racial problems at school. The majority of these problems were name calling, insults, and interpersonal fights. Racial and ethnic attitudes toward other groups appear to indicate tolerance among the vast majority of students. There was little evidence of entrenched negative attitudes toward any group, though African Americans were ranked slightly lower than other racial groups. By far the most tolerant groups of students were the youth of mixed racial or ethnic background and Pacific Islander youth.

These results confirm the observations of the P.R.O.P.S. members of the school's social ecology of intergroup relations. There exist a number of separate communities within Mission High School that are organized along cultural lines. A significant number of students cross these lines in their personal associations. There is no sign of ongoing intergroup tension or conflict. Rather, there is a lack of contact and knowledge of different groups for the majority of students, particularly incoming 9th graders and newly arrived immigrants. It is significant that there is no racial or ethnic group that clearly holds a numerical or status advantage in the school. There are few whites and the diversity of the school diffuses issues of power, control, and privilege. This may change with the new administration, which is developing most of the school's services and culture directed at the Latino students and families. The P.R.O.P.S. members concluded that efforts to improve intergroup relations at Mission High School had great possibilities for success.

Programmatic/Policy Implications: The P.R.O.P.S. program relies on its core group of students to set up a dynamic that will affect the entire school population. Student members of the P.R.O.P.S. Program benefit directly from the training in research and community organizing that they receive. Students are chosen based on a combination of criteria including leadership ability, status and standing among marginalized groups of students within the school community, and marginal academic performance. The school community benefits from the program as well.

The project is based on the premise that the crucial arena for a change in race relations is the community and/or school (as a kind of community), not individual by individual. It is a systemic change at the community level that propels changes in group dynamics. Rather than developing a curriculum geared toward individual attitudinal change, the core goal of the

P.R.O.P.S. program is to develop a methodology that helps people understand the dynamics of their situation and find ways to direct those dynamics toward positive ends. Young people are the best resource for improving intergroup relations among adolescents. Youth-driven and youth-run programs that aim at changing the cultural environment of their school or community have tremendous potential for affecting the attitudes of a large number of youth and changing the context and environment in which they interact into one which facilitates contact and cooperation.

Contact:
Howard Pinderhughes
Assistant Professor
Department of Social & Behavioral Sciences
University of California, San Francisco
Box 0612, N631G
San Francisco, CA 94143
415-502-5074
415-476-6552 (fax)
Email: hpinder@itsa.ucsf.edu

Project Title: Ethnic Identity, Bicultural Self-Efficacy, and Intergroup Conflict and Violence

---

Principal Investigator: Fernando Soriano

Purpose: The purpose of this study was to examine the relationship between psychosocial and cultural factors acting as potential mediators of intercultural group conflict among adolescents. In keeping with Albert Bandura's social cognitive learning model, this project examined the following contexts: (1) group and contextual influences (i.e., group conditions that promote positive intergroup relations); (2) cognitive processes, including developmental processes (i.e., identity and cultural identity formation); and (3) behavioral skills (i.e., social skills for effective interpersonal and intercultural interactions, including bicultural self-efficacy). Key study questions included: To what extent are cultural factors, such as ethnic identity and bicultural self-efficacy, related to intercultural group relations and social problems, such as violence and aggression? If cultural factors are enhanced, will intercultural group conflict be reduced, as well as social problem behaviors, such as violence and aggression?

Methodology: The study population consisted mainly of adolescent males ages 13 to 18 who resided in two northern Californian counties and who attended California "court schools." Most were wards of the court, on probation and/or resided in restricted residential placements. The northern California counties were selected because they encompassed large culturally diverse populations. This project had both research and intervention components divided into two phases, one for each year of the project. Phase I activities centered on conducting a survey of 481 adolescents representing largely the targeted youth population of concern. The purpose of this survey was to assess and ascertain the relationship between cultural factors (i.e., ethnic identity, bicultural self-efficacy, and acculturation) and outcome measures, such as intercultural group attitudes and behavior, in the hypothesized direction. These data also served as a means of assessing baseline conditions on independent variables, which helped in the development of curriculum for the school-based intervention of focus in Phase II (year two).

In Phase II of the project, 86 adolescents from the same population took part in programmatic activities. A total of 48 youths from 3 schools comprised an experimental group, while 38 were from two comparable schools, which served as a control group. Youths in the experimental groups were assigned to culturally balanced subgroups (about 15) in classrooms led by a program leader and a trained teacher. These groups took part in a 16-week, 3-component program that addressed: (1) individual enhancement training (including interpersonal relations, communication skills, goal setting, and conflict resolution skill training), (2) cultural training (cultural awareness and sensitivity, bicultural self-efficacy, intercultural group relations, and cultural identity training), and (3) community-bonding training components (through community service projects).

Key/Major Findings: Results from the survey in Phase I indicated a clear relationship between cultural measures and intercultural group relations and social problems, such as violence. That is, the data showed that both negative intercultural group attitudes and self-reported behaviors were inversely related to ethnic identity and bicultural self-efficacy.

Results for the intervention demonstrated a more complex relationship between variables and individuals. The relatively small number of participants in the intervention, plus difficulty in securing a more clearly comparable control group, made it difficult to reveal a clearer relationship between the variables as expected. Even with such difficulty, the results did suggest that the program is efficacious in diminishing intercultural group conflict and in reducing violence and aggression.

Programmatic/Policy Implications: The results of the project pointed to the great need that culturally diverse adolescents have for information that validates their cultural heritage and background. Also evident was their need for enhancing their ethnic identity and for increasing their intercultural communication and relationship skills. This has implications for school curriculum serving culturally diverse students. This was one of the first studies to demonstrate that the increase in ethnic pride and identity does not necessarily lead to intercultural group conflict. The results further validate the importance of training to increase the capacity of adolescents to handle interpersonal conflict challenges both within and outside of school grounds.

Schools should consider increasing the exposure of adolescents to information validating their own cultural backgrounds and those of other cultural groups, while also improving their intercultural communication and relationship skills. While many schools may be multicultural in composition, too many students feel alienated and threatened by culturally different populations. In particular, it is important to consider increasing organized opportunities for adolescent students to interact and develop relationships with those outside of their cultural groups. More research needs to be encouraged to more carefully examine the relationship between cultural factors, such as ethnic identity and bicultural self-efficacy, and social problems, such as intercultural group relations and social problems among high-risk adolescents (e.g., violence and aggression).

Contact:

Fernando I. Soriano
San Diego State University
8522 Neva Avenue
San Diego, CA 92123
619-495-7703 x3585
619-495-7704 (fax)
Email: fsoriano@sunstroke.sdsu.edu

Project Title: From Intolerance to Understanding: A Study of Intergroup Relations Among High School Youth

---

Principal Investigator: Hanh Cao Yu

Purpose: The purpose of the study, *From Intolerance to Understanding,* is to expand knowledge of racial and ethnic borders created by differences in the attitudes and behaviors across students' multiple worlds and identify effective school approaches that foster intergroup understanding and border crossing. The study examined the impact of the school interventions on intergroup relations among high school students. The key research questions were as follows:

1. How do family values, peer norms, and school context influence students' identity development, border-crossing abilities, and relations with youths of different backgrounds?
2. How do systematic school strategies designed to improve intergroup relations foster border-crossings, increased opportunities to interact, and the identification of commonalties? From the students' perspective, which school strategies are most effective in promoting their ability to relate to youth of different backgrounds?

The study built on the Students' Multiple Worlds (SMW) model, which is a theoretical model of the interrelationships between students' family, peer, and school worlds, examining in particular how meanings and understandings derived from these worlds combine to affect students' engagement with schools and learning. The SMW model directs attention to the nature of boundaries and borders as well as processes of movement among different worlds.

Methodology: This multifaceted three-year research study involves two phases of data collection from 1996 to 1999. Key elements of our approach included:

• Selecting three pairs of matched high schools from urban and suburban districts and conducting 5 rounds of site visits that focus on schools' and individuals' experiences in the matched schools. School- and student-level issues we examined included the genesis and evolution of the schools' programs, policies, philosophies, and practices as well as factors that influence how students developed their group identities and how they reacted to the schools' efforts to improve intergroup relationships (72 students interviewed).

- Conducting 4 focus groups with single-race/ethnic groups at each school.

- Conducting a quantitative survey of the class of 2000 in the 6 matched schools, in which we asked about students' attitudes and behavior toward different ethnic groups (approximately 2,300 students were surveyed).

Key/Major Findings: We have found three emerging patterns of how schools are addressing intergroup relations and promoting racial harmony. These different approaches include passive, reactive, and proactive measures to creating conditions for students to explore their ethnic identity and to set the norms and rules of behavior for intergroup interactions. The "passive" school is characterized by lack of widespread acknowledgement that intergroup tensions exist on campus and few, if any, programs are implemented with the expressed purpose of directly promoting intergroup contact. "Reactive" schools are responding to a history of interracial strife and external political pressures exerted by community members to address issues of equity and racial conflict on their campuses. These schools have a litany of multicultural and diversity training programs that have heightened students' awareness of their own ethnic identity and the segregation at their school. Finally, "proactive" schools have engaged in promoting positive intergroup contact simply as an expression of their recognition of the importance of creating a healthy, personalized environment for students to learn and connect with other students and adults.

In our cross-analyses of students' case studies, we discovered distinctive patterns among students as they cross various social settings to form relationships with peers of diverse backgrounds. We use a typology to illustrate four primary patterns.

Typology of Student Intergroup Border Crossing:

- Type I: Heterogeneous peer groups/Border crossings smooth
- Type II: Transitional peer groups/Border crossings managed
- Type III: Homogeneous peer groups/Border crossing resisted
- Type IV: Heterogeneous peer groups/Limited border crossing

Students from each type had influential factors that enhanced or limited their experiences across their family, school, and peer contexts. We also found that border crossings can only be achieved under certain circumstances, and in some cases, movement across worlds can cause great inner conflict as students reorient themselves in each setting. School structures can greatly determine the kinds of interactions students can be expected to achieve. Students reported that participating in diverse classroom environments and extracurricular activities increased their interaction with different social and ethnic groups.

Programmatic/Policy Implications: Based on an examination of six diverse schools throughout California, it is evident that most schools in the study are no longer maintaining a passive stance toward increasingly diverse student bodies. School leaders, teachers, parents, and students are beginning to challenge traditional policies and practices that lead to inequitable treatment of students of color, and more schools appear to be adopting a reactive or proactive approach to addressing barriers to harmonious intergroup relations.

Policy makers need to understand that there is no one predetermined pathway or set of strategies for schools to follow to address racism and promote positive intergroup interactions. Positive intergroup relations can be achieved through strategies that seek to enhance students identity, development, and learning experiences. While some schools have heightened students' levels of awareness of their ethnic identity and of issues of race to create a more meaningful context for students to interact, school-wide efforts may not be effective unless they take into account students' varying needs and levels of readiness to grapple with issues of intergroup relations, as indicated by the different "types" they represent.

There are also several major implications for intergroup relations program design and policy from the emerging patterns of student border crossings:

• Programs must take into account the diversity of the types of students' experiences, backgrounds, stages of identity development, and supports available from family, peers, and school. For example:

—Students of color are often the target of inconsistent tracking and disciplinary policies and general societal discrimination.

—White students have been conditioned not to speak about race and power dynamics. However, they are experiencing a greater sense of alienation in increasingly diverse learning environments.

• Types IV and II need added support for their identity development and affirmation of who they are so that they do not feel the need to hide their racial and ethnic selves.

- Type II students need safe spaces to explore common fears, perceptions, and understandings, and to exchange coping strategies.

Contact:

Hanh Cao Yu
Social Policy Research Associates
1330 Broadway, Suite 1426
Oakland, CA 94612
510-763-1499
510-763-1599 (fax)
Email: hanh_cao_yu@spra.com

Project Title: Improving Intergroup Relations Among Youth Through Understanding Cross-Cultural Differences in Basic Value Orientations

Principal Investigator: Patricia Marks Greenfield

Purpose: This project explores the influence of young people's cultural values, as acquired at home, on their relationship with youth from different backgrounds in the context of school sports teams. This project has particular importance because (1) school is a setting in which much intergroup contact occurs; (2) sports teams are one of the few school contexts in which various groups work together as equals for common goals; and (3) there has been a dearth of research on the role of cultural values in intergroup relations among youth.

Methodology: During the year ending June 30, 1998, we completed baseline data collection on intergroup relations on eight multiethnic high school sports teams. All data have been entered into a unified electronic database. Our design includes four basketball and four volleyball teams from two schools, evenly split between boys' and girls' teams. Each team has members of three or four major ethnic groups playing together on the same team: African American, Asian American, Latino, and Euro-American.

A multimethod technique was used to collect the data for this study. That is, the perspectives of both research observers and sports team members were acquired, as was quantitative data from questionnaire responses. Incidents or issues that are described by more than one team member can be used to analyze and understand differing cultural interpretations of the same event. This yields an important database of contrasting cultural interpretations of the same interpersonal issues. The three methods used in this study are ethnographic participant observation, student journals, and assessment of individualistic and collectivistic values.

Key/Major Findings: The study found that the best (statistically significant) prediction concerning roles in a conflict was provided by the participants' collectivism scores in the value assessment. That is, in 78 percent of the conflicts, the team member who had scored the most collectivistic of the pair on the assessment took the collectivistic position in the real-world conflict, while the teammate who had scored as less collectivistic took the individualistic position in the real-world conflict.

We think that collectivism scores may have predicted positions in actual individualism-collectivism conflicts better than individualism scores because there is more variability in collectivistic values in an individualistic society such as the United States: whereas everyone gets exposure to individualistic values, exposure to collectivistic values is more limited to particular subcultures.

We also found that the value scores of the participants in a conflict predicted their roles in that conflict better than their parents' value scores did. We interpret this to mean that teenagers' behavior in interpersonal situations is not a direct reflection of their parents' values. Their parents' values have been interpreted through the lens of their own personalities, situations, and developmental stage, and this process leads to value transformation, reflected in the teenagers' own value scores. It was these—specifically the collectivism scores—that best predicted their own value positions in actual conflict situations.

There was an association between ethnicity and value orientation. Most of the time, Asian Americans took the collectivistic position in an intergroup conflict; most of the time, Euro-Americans took the individualistic position. This ethnic patterning was as expected. Latinos, expected to be collectivistic, took individualistic positions less frequently than did Euro-Americans, but they also took collectivistic positions less frequently than did Asian Americans. This latter pattern was not expected; we will be looking to see if it holds in a larger sample of data.

Programmatic/Policy Implications: These multiethnic teams' experiences of conflict and misunderstanding reflect the misunderstandings that occur in society as a whole. The different perspectives that were heard by means of our multivocal methodology have provided us with solid evidence of the players' perceptions of intergroup and interpersonal issues in their own words. The method of multivocal ethnography has been successful in revealing different cultural voices in situations of interpersonal and intergroup conflict.

In Phase 2 of the study, we completed an intervention with two girls' basketball teams that we had previously studied. We tried to use what we had learned about value-based conflict in Phase I of the project to improve intergroup understanding and harmony within each team. Some preliminary results will be available in the next few months.

Contact:
Patricia Marks Greenfield
Department of Psychology
University of California, Los Angeles
405 Hilgard Avenue
Los Angeles, CA 90095
310-825-7526
310-206-5895 (fax)

Project Title: Immigrant and Native Minority Adolescent Interaction: Miami

Principal Investigator: Alex Stepick

Purpose: The project focused on interethnic relations among native and immigrant minority youth in the Miami metropolitan area of Dade County, Florida, primarily in four high schools with cohorts of youth from particular ethnic groups—African American, Haitian, English-speaking West Indian, Cuban, Nicaraguan, or Mexican. The goal was to understand first the nature of relations among these different native and immigrant minority groups and second to examine what factors in their day-to-day interactions promote or deter positive intergroup relations.

Methodology: The study began when the cohorts entered their first year of high school; they now have graduated, dropped out, or are on the verge of graduation. The research includes three methods: (1) longitudinal participant observation of youth in the schools, their homes, and their communities; (2) intensive interviews (both surveys and open-ended) of the youth, school personnel, parents, and other adults who work with the communities' youth; and (3) focus groups of youths.

Key/Major Findings: The most important findings of this study include:

1. Contemporary immigration has altered interethnic relations in the United States:

a. Conflict does occur between and among immigrant groups and between immigrants and native-born Americans.

b. The most common conflict is between newcomers who may not speak American English or know American ways and established residents, including immigrants who have linguistically and culturally assimilated.

c. Low-income immigrants settling in inner cities display segmentary assimilation to one of America's two racial/ethnic minority groups—African Americans or Latinos—not to generic, mainstream white culture. Immigrant youth do assimilate rapidly—some too rapidly for their parents' tastes. Yet immigrant youth styles are likely to mirror those of the peers with whom they have the greatest contact. Nevertheless, assimilated immigrant youth recognize that they are not fully American and thus identify as a "hyphenated American," such as Haitian American or Cuban American, rather than simply American or African American or Latino.

2. There is a disjuncture between kids' concerns and adult perceptions of kids' most important problems. Much of the conflict that occurs is rooted in the tensions of American youth peer culture, such as gender relations and friendship cliques. Yet, in multiethnic environments it assumes and often manifests itself as an ethnic conflict.

3. The main tenets of the contact hypothesis remain true, but schools seldom fulfill the hypothesis's prerequisites, particularly that of equal status contact. Also, the debate over multiculturalism misses the mark. Institutions should not promote either multicultural events or "American" cultural. In multicultural environments, institutions should promote both.

a. Multicultural activities, particularly those that positively highlight marginalized minorities, best address the requirement of effecting equal status.

b. Activities that distinguish minority groups must be complemented by other activities that require cooperation and thus effect solidarity across all groups.

Programmatic/Policy Implications: The culturally specific events provide minority groups with the opportunity and the material to positively evaluate themselves and thus to feel that they are the equal of the majority population. Conservative critics of multiculturalism assert that it divides the population and undermines cross-group solidarity. This research, however, indicates that specific celebrations of minority culture are a necessary prerequisite for bringing adolescents together on an equal footing. To achieve positive interactions, however, activities that spotlight separate cultures must first be more than symbolic shadows reluctantly performed and second must be complemented by other activities that fulfill the contact hypothesis's requirement of cooperation.

While we continue to examine multiculturalism and equal status, our tentative conclusion is that unity can be accomplished while still promoting multicultural activities. The goal is not, however, easy to achieve. Administrators and teachers must genuinely promote both the multicultural and the unifying activities. Students are especially adept at detecting insincerity. Otherwise, this issue become another example of a disjuncture between adolescents' and adults' interests and perceptions.

Contact:
Alex Stepick
Director, Immigration & Ethnicity Institute
Florida International University
Miami, FL 33199
305-348-2247
305-348-3605 (fax)
Email: stepick@Fiu.edu

Project Title: Improving Intergroup Relations Through Students' Behavioral Journalism

Principal Investigator: Alfred L. McAlister

Purpose: Behavioral journalism influences audiences by presenting peer modeling for cognitive processes that lead to behavior change. To investigate whether students' behavioral journalism can change attitudes related to intergroup hostility, a quasi-experimental research project was carried out among two multicultural Houston high school populations. The technique used student newsletters to promote improved intergroup relations among 91 high school students in two Houston schools.

Methodology: Sharpstown High School was selected as the program school because of its very high level of diversity compared to other schools in the district. Its population is multicultural with no group in the majority. Another of the more diverse schools was selected as a comparison, although it was larger and had a higher proportion of Hispanic students. In the program school, a survey was conducted in early December 1996 and late May 1997. A survey was also conducted in the comparison school in June 1997. Reading questions from printed questionnaires, students answered questions concerning conflict resolution, group relations and other topics. To protect the confidentiality of respondents and avoid the low response rate that would result from requiring signed parental consent, students did not provide identifying information on the surveys.

Key/Major Findings: The differences between intergroup attitudes and intentions in the baseline, follow-up, and comparison groups are generally consistent with the hypothesized effect of vicarious "extended contact" provided through students' behavioral journalism. Willingness for intergroup affiliation at school was significantly increased, and there is strong evidence for an effect on attitudes toward intermarriage. Perceptions of intergroup similarity were also increased. Effects on superiority beliefs and sympathy for other groups were small and not consistently significant. The campaign evidently was effective in promoting moral engagement by changing beliefs about the acceptability of violence, with changes coming mainly among those with the most aggressive attitudes. Although the peer modeling stories in the newsletters demonstrated skills for intergroup communication, these were not measured. Instruments for assessing self-efficacy for intergroup communication should be included in future studies of this technique. The reduced intentions for intergroup hostility among students at Sharpstown High School suggest that the cognitive effects were sufficient to achieve a moderate reduction in the likelihood of discriminatory behaviors.

Programmatic/Policy Implications: Despite their shortcomings, the data presented provide evidence that students' behavioral journalism can be used to promote tolerance and prevent intergroup hostility. Further application and testing is clearly warranted. The newsletter approach, with university students distributing stories about how young people successfully cope with diversity, was feasible and well accepted by the high school student audience. We are presently training Sharpstown students to produce and distribute newsletters themselves, with further follow-up and replication in the comparison school. During future years we plan to expand the "Students for Peace" campaign throughout the Houston school district and to other interested communities. Because of its flexibility and convenience for mass application, this method can efficiently reach diverse communities in large populations.

Contact:
Alfred L. McAlister
Behavioral Sciences
University of Texas, School of Public Health
2609 University Avenue
Austin, TX 78705
512-471-5801
512-471-8635 (fax)
Email: alfred.mcalister@ktl.f1atmcimail

Project Title: Improving Interethnic Relations Among Youth: A School-Based Project Involving Teachers, Parents, and Children

Principal Investigators: Beverly Daniel Tatum and Phyllis C. Brown

Purpose: School-based efforts to improve intergroup relations among youth are usually focused directly on the young people themselves, ignoring the potentially critical influence that teachers' and parents' attitudes and actions may have on student behavior. This two-year project investigated the combined effect on young people's intergroup relations of interventions involving teachers, students, and parents in a small Northeastern school district with an increasing school population of color (presently 24 percent). In particular, the project was designed to facilitate the positive development of racial/ethnic identity not only for adolescents, but also for the adult educators who work with them and the parents who hope to guide them through this developmental period.

Methodology: The first component focused on the development of adolescents' racial/ethnic identity as a strategy for improving intergroup relations. Approximately 50 middle school students from six racial/ethnic groups (Latino, African-American, Asian Pacific American, European-American, Jewish, and biracial) were recruited each year to participate in an after-school Cultural Identity Group (CIG) program. The program consisted of weekly small-group discussions held over a 16-week period, first in same-race and later in "blended" groups. The groups provided the opportunity to discuss the impact of race and racism, to explore one's own sense of race and ethnicity and that of others. The impact of the groups was measured with the use of pre- and post-administration of Jean Phinney's Multiethnic Identity Measure, and through the use of interviews with a representative sample (39) of the CIG group participants.

The second component of the intervention consisted of a semester-long professional development course that required participants to examine closely their own sense of ethnic and racial identity and their attitudes toward other groups, as well as develop effective antiracist curricula and educational practices that will be affirming of student identities. It is assumed that teachers must look at their own racial identity in order to be able to support the positive development of their students' racial/ethnic identities. They must also be able to engage in racial dialogue themselves in order to facilitate student conversation.

The course was offered four times over the two-year period, and 83 teachers from the district participated. Data sources for the evaluation of this component included ethnographic observations recorded by an ethnographer, the reflection papers and action plans produced by the participants over the course of the semester, and pre- and post-interviews with a subset (14) of participating educators.

The third component involved a series of parent meetings designed to provide the parents of middle school students with information about adolescent identity development and intergroup relations in the school, to encourage positive intergroup interactions among adults as a way of modeling desirable behavior, and to serve as a way of identifying parent and community resources who might help with the CIG project. Data collection was limited to parent evaluations of the workshop series, which were very positive.

Key/Major Findings: Along with apparent shifts in racial awareness and sense of racial identity (as revealed in interviews and reflection papers), there were also shifts in classroom practice (as revealed in an analysis of the action plans). A total of 56 percent involved efforts to make the curriculum more inclusive of people of color; 30 percent focused on improving relationships between teachers and parents or students of color; and 14 percent involved efforts to change institutional policies and practices, such as tracking and monolingual assessment procedures.

Programmatic/Policy Implications: In order to interrupt the cycle of racism in society, young people need an understanding of how prejudice and racism have operated to divide us from one another. They also need to feel empowered to do something about it. Opportunities to discuss race, ethnicity, and oppression in a safe environment should be available to young people, especially in school.

However, many adults, including educators, are both uncomfortable and unskilled in how to talk about racial issues with children. Many teachers have had limited opportunity to explore these issues as part of their own educational experience, and as a consequence, hesitate to lead discussions about racial tensions in society for fear that they will generate classroom conflict. Unfortunately, when school personnel avoid a proactive examination of racial issues, they may find themselves trying to manage crisis situations as the result of erupting racial tensions. Increasingly, incidents of racial intolerance and hostility at all age levels are being reported in schools.

It should be clear that avoidance of race-related discussions is not the answer. Yet too many teachers are clearly confused about how to proceed.

Our data suggest that young people and adults alike need and benefit from "safe spaces" to explore personal attitudes and to reflect upon their own and others' racial and ethnic identity. Creating such opportunities can have a positive impact on interethnic relations in schools.

Contact:
Beverly Daniel Tatum
Dean of the College
Mount Holyoke College
202 Mary Lyon Hall
South Hadley, MA 01075
413-538-2481
413-538-3059 (fax)
Email: BTatum@MTHolyoke.edu

Project Title: Gender and Race Work in an Urban Magnet School

Principal Investigators: Lois Weis, Michele Fine, and Linda Powell

Purpose: In this project, we seek to understand personal biographies of race/ethnicity and cross-racial relations of youths and adults (gathered in individual and focus group interviews) and to explicate the structural conditions of three interracial communities. Through observation, interviews, and document collection, we attempted to demystify the process by which adults and youths interact in such settings. It is important that we not portray these settings as though they were simply free of adult intervention—to do so would be to erase the powerful presence that adults have in establishing and permitting "safety zones" in which interracial relations can grow and be nourished. Thus, we have chosen sites in which we know that adults are working, across racial and ethnic groups and self-consciously, on creating "free spaces" for youths to come together intellectually, aesthetically, and politically. We conducted interviews and observations in order to understand how such spaces are constructed, secured, sabotaged, resurrected, and maintained over time. Delineating these critical elements allowed us both to theorize about racial identities and cross-racial and ethnic relations among youths, and to develop for practitioners some frameworks within which they, too, can imagine and create such spaces.

Methodology: Michelle Fine conducted research inside a 9th grade classroom within an integrated public school, in which students across racial, ethnic, and class backgrounds come together in a world literature course. The faculty—one African American man and one white woman—collaborate regularly to sustain intellectually and politically rich classes. The focus is on desegregated classrooms and detracking.

Linda Powell conducted research within a professional development setting for urban teachers engaging in "family group" and analyzed individual and group interviews with teachers.

Lois Weis worked with a group of racially mixed 9th and 12th grade girls, who are participating in the program in an arts-based urban magnet school in Buffalo. The program, called My Bottom Line, is an abstinence-based sex education program that wanders through enormously interesting issues regarding body image, sexuality, and gender roles in U.S. society for a full semester. She interviewed young women as to their experiences in this group as well as broader issues concerning race and gender within the contexts of intergroup relations in the 1990s.

Key/Major Findings:[1]   Participant observation and interview data were gathered during spring semester 1997 at a magnet school (grades 5-12) geared toward the arts in Buffalo, New York. The school is highly mixed ethnically and racially, having 45 percent white, 45 percent African American, 8 percent Latino/Latina, 1 percent First Nations People, and 1 percent Asian students.

The officially stated goal of My Bottom Line is "to prevent or delay the onset of sexual activity, build self esteem and increase self sufficiency in young women through an abstinence based, gender specific prevention education program." Students voluntarily attend the program during study hall, participating one or two times a week. The expressed intent of the group is one of encouraging abstinence among girls who are not yet sexually active. The site, in addition to dealing with issues of sexual abstinence, was intentionally established in order to empower young women, particularly in their relationships with young men. The adults in charge explain that women's bodies must be under the control of women themselves and should not be a site for male control, abuse, or exploitation. In addition, the program provided participants a space within which personal and collective identity formation across racial and ethnic lines potentially takes place. The study assessed the extent to which this space offers a "home" within which social stereotypes are contested and new identities tried on.

Programmatic/Policy Implications: In this program, young women traverse a variety of subjects regarding race, gender, sexuality, and men. Moving through these issues, they begin to form a new collective based on a stronger woman/girl, one who is different in many ways from those left behind emotionally in the neighborhood. It is a collective that surges across racial groups, although not necessarily in terms of intimate friendships. But these young women, nevertheless, share the most intimate pieces of themselves in the group setting, creating a form of friendship that may or may not transcend the bounds of the school, or even the group. They think the group gives them the space they need to think things out—to live life differently than those they feel are destined to failure.

---

[1]These findings refer specifically to the work of Lois Weis, who participated in the workshop.

Data suggest that this program offers a powerful space for revising gender and ethnic racial subjectivities as students gain a set of lenses and allies for social critiques. Students "bear secrets," doing so across racial and ethnic lines, setting the stage for cross-race/cross ethnic interactions around important issues in the future, in spite of the limited purpose under which the group was initially formed.

Contact:

Lois Weis
Organization Administration and Policy
State University of New York, Buffalo
468 Baldy Hall
Buffalo, NY 14260
716-645-6626
716-645-2481 (fax)
Email: Weis@acsu.Buffalo.edu

Project Title: Early Adolescent Development Study

Principal Investigator: Diane Hughes

Purpose: The Early Adolescent Development Study is a two-year short-term longitudinal study focusing on intergroup relations, school experiences, and psychosocial adjustment among a sample of 991 elementary and middle school youth (531 white, 400 African American, 29 Hispanic, and 31 Asian or Asian American). The study focuses primarily on elaborating developmental and social factors that facilitate or impede positive intergroup friendships during middle childhood. By following students over a two-year period, we were aiming to examine the extent to which there were shifts in children's orientations toward same-race and other-race peers over the course of several ecological transitions, including that from elementary to middle school in 5th grade and that from heterogeneous to formally tracked classrooms in 6th grade.

Methodology: The program was designed to follow longitudinally a relatively large sample of youth attending 3rd through 5th grades in an integrated suburban school district in the Northeast. Several characteristics of the schools and of the district were of particular importance in the design and conceptualization of the study. First, whereas the two middle schools (housing the 5th grade students) were racially balanced, reflecting the overall population of the district (about 50 percent European American, 40 percent African American, and 10 percent children of other ethnic backgrounds) the elementary schools (housing the 3rd and 4th graders) varied in racial composition. Two elementary schools were predominantly (56 percent) African American schools, one elementary school was predominantly (61 percent) European American, and two of the elementary schools were racially balanced. Moreover, whereas school policy dictated heterogeneous ability grouping among 3rd, 4th, and 5th graders, students were tracked within homogeneous classrooms in 6th grade.

Key/Major Findings: With the exception of 3rd grade African American students, a greater proportion of students reported same-race as compared to other-race friendships. In addition, across all grades, white students were more likely to report same-race friends and less likely to report other-race friends than were their African American counterparts. However, whereas white students' friendship patterns were relatively stable across time, African American students showed an increasing tendency toward same-race peers. For instance, 45 percent of African American 3rd grade students as compared to 70 percent of African American 5th grade students reported that "many" or "all" of their friends were from their racial group. The shift away from other-race friends was less dramatic but significant nevertheless: 45 percent of African American 3rd grade students as compared with 30 percent of African American 5th grade students reported that "all" or "many" of their friends were a different race from themselves. In a school district that is fully integrated, one would expect about equal numbers of students reporting same-race and other-race friendships. Clearly, then, race is an important basis upon which student's friendship choices are made.

Again, findings indicate greater same-race peer preference, and greater stability over time, among white as compared to African American students. Analyses also suggested that the most dramatic shift toward same-race peer relationships over time was evidenced within the subsample of students who were in 3rd grade during year one of the study.

Finally, we examined relationships between parents' reports about their communications to children about race and children's reports about their peer relationships. Although children are exposed to, and absorb, messages about race from many sources, including teachers, the media, community members, and others, parental attitudes and messages are likely to exert an especially powerful influence on children's attitudes toward their own and other ethnic groups. Parents transmit these attitudes to children intentionally and inadvertently by way of implicit and explicit messages encoded in their ongoing interactions with their children.

Programmatic/Policy Implications: In many ways, the findings regarding children's peer preferences raise more questions than they answer. These findings support findings from other studies regarding the prevalence of same-race peer preferences. In general, student reports about their peer relationships and contacts suggest an overwhelming preference for same-race peers among a substantial majority of youth. Although age-related increases in same-race peer preference were evident in cross-sectional and longitudinal analyses, these were much less pronounced and nonsignificant when differences in school racial composition were accounted for.

Among African American students, a variety of individual and ecological factors were associated with patterns of peer preference. African American students who identified more strongly with their racial group and actively engaged in information-seeking about race reported more same-race and fewer other-race friendships. Perceived unfair treatment was also associated with African American and white students' peer preferences, as was their gender. Not surprisingly, parental socialization messages were quite strongly associated with African American students' peer preference patterns.

Perhaps the most puzzling aspect has been the absence of a relationship between proposed predictor variables and peer preference patterns within the subsample of white students. This is undoubtedly due, in part, to the relative lack of variation in these students peer preferences. The overwhelming majority of them reported many same-race and few other-race peer choices. Planned analyses of school structural variables and classroom pedagogical practices as reported by teachers may add additional insight into these phenomena.

Contact:

Diane Hughes
Psychology Department
New York University
6 Washington Place, Rm. 280, 2nd Floor
New York, NY 10003
212-998-7906
212-995-4018 (fax)
Email: Hughes@xp.psych.nyu.edu

APPENDIX

B

Workshop on Research to Improve Intergroup Relations Among Youth

NOVEMBER 9-10, 1998

Agenda

Monday, November 9

8:30 - 9:00   Continental Breakfast

9:00 - 9:15   **Opening Remarks and Overview**

David A. Hamburg,
Chair, Forum on Adolescence

Michele D. Kipke
Director, Board on Children, Youth, and Families

9:15 - 10:00   **Morning Keynote Presentations**

Changing America: Indicators of Well-Being and Disparities in the United States
Rebecca Blank, Council of Economic Advisers

Developmental Perspectives on Racial Identity Among Youth
Margaret Beale Spencer, University of Pennsylvania

10:00 - 10:15   **Overview of the Research to Improve Intergroup
                   Relations Among Youth Initiative Funded by
                   Carnegie Corporation of New York**
                   Vivien Stewart, Carnegie Corporation of New York

10:15 -11:45   **Panel 1: Research Findings: Cultural Values, Toler-
                   ance, and Intergroup Relations**

                   Panel Participants:
                   Diane Hughes, New York University
                   Patricia Marks Greenfield, University of California
                   Alex Stepick, Florida International University
                   Hanh Cao Yu, Social Policy Research Associates

                   Discussant:
                   Camille Zubrinsky Charles, University of Pennsylvania

                   Selected Questions and Comments from the Audience
                   and General Discussion

11:45 - 12:45   Lunch

12:45 - 2:15   **Panel 2: Research Findings: Interventions Designed
                   to Promote Intergroup Relations**

                   Panel Participants:
                   Sherryl Browne Graves, Hunter College of the City
                   University of New York
                   Ron Slaby, Education Development Center
                   Dennis Barr, Harvard University
                   Phyllis Katz, Institute for Research on Social Problems

                   Discussant:
                   Robert Selman, Harvard University
                   Generalizing and Sustaining Success

                   Selected Questions and Comments from the Audience
                   and General Discussion

2:15 - 2:30   Break

2:30 - 3:15   **A Research Conference on Racial Trends in the United States: Key Findings Related to Intergroup Relations Among Youth[1]**

                  Faith Mitchell
                  Director, Division on Social and Economic Studies

                  Selected Questions and Comments from the Audience and General Discussion

3:15 - 4:00   **Building a Research Agenda to Promote Peaceful, Respectful Relations Among Children and Adolescents**

                  Ruby Takanishi
                  Executive Director, Foundation for Child Development

                  Selected Questions and Comments from the Audience and General Discussion

4:15 - 5:30   Reception, Auditorium Gallery

Tuesday, November 10

8:30 - 9:00   Continental Breakfast

9:00 - 9:15   **Opening Remarks**

                  David Hamburg
                  Michele Kipke

---

[1]This conference was convened by the Commission on Behavioral and Social Sciences and Education of the National Research Council in Washington, DC, on October 15-16, 1998.

9:15 - 10:45   **Panel 3: Research Findings: Cultural Values, Citizenship, and Intergroup Relations**

Panel Presentations:
Constance A. Flanagan, Pennsylvania State University
Cindy Carlson, University of Texas, Austin
Michele Foster, Claremont University Center and Graduate School
Lois Weis, State University of New York

Discussant:
Eugene Garcia, University of California, Berkeley

Selected Questions and Comments from the Audience and General Discussion

10:45- 11:00   Break

11:00 - 12:15   **Panel 4: Research Findings: Interventions Designed to Promote Intergroup Relations**

Panel Presentations:
Fernando Soriano, Education Training Research Associates, San Diego State University
Alfred McAlister, University of Texas
Howard Pinderhughes, University of California, San Francisco
Beverly Daniel Tatum, Mount Holyoke College
Phyllis Brown, Lesley College

Discussant:
Kenyon Chan, Loyola Marymount University
Generalizing and Sustaining Success

Selected Questions and Comments from the Audience and General Discussion

12:15 - 12:30   **Closing Remarks**

David A. Hamburg

12:30   Adjourn

Selected Reports of the Board on Children, Youth, and Families

Risks and Opportunities: Synthesis of Studies on Adolescence (1999)

Adolescent Development and the Biology of Puberty: Summary of a Workshop on New Research (1999)

Adolescent Decision-Making: Implications for Prevention Programs: Summary of a Workshop (1999)

Revisiting Home Visiting Summary of a Workshop (1999)

Protecting Youth at Work: Health, Safety, and Development of Working Children and Adolescents in the United States (1998)

America's Children: Health Insurance and Access to Care (with the IOM Division of Health Care Services) (1998)

Systems of Accountability: Implementing Children's Health Insurance Programs (with the IOM Division of Health Care Services) (1998)

Longitudinal Surveys of Children: Report of a Workshop (with the NRC Committee on National Statistics) (1998)

From Generation to Generation: The Health and Well-Being of Children in Immigrant Families (1998)

New Findings on Poverty and Child Health and Nutrition: Summary of a Research Briefing (1998)

Violence in Families: Assessing Treatment and Prevention Programs (1998)

Welfare, the Family, and Reproductive Behavior: Report of a Meeting (with the NRC Committee on Population) (1998)

Educating Language-Minority Children (1998)

Improving Schooling for Language-Minority Children: A Research Agenda (1997)

New Findings on Welfare and Children's Development: Summary of a Research Briefing (1997)

Youth Development and Neighborhood Influences: Challenges and Opportunities: Summary of a Workshop (1996)

Paying Attention to Children in a Changing Health Care System: Summaries of Workshops (1996)

Integrating Federal Statistics on Children (with the NRC Committee on National Statistics) (1995)